T...

HILAIRE BELLOC, gran... ...ait
painter, was born near ... ...ght up
largely in Sussex by his En... ...self famed as
a feminist author. His var... ...stic career began
even before he finished his Fi... national service in the
1890s (he founded his own paper—*The Paternoster
Review*), and ended, effectively, as a *Sunday Times*
columnist during the Second World War. He was by
turns well known as a comic versifier, a serious poet, a
novelist, a biographer, a Member of Parliament, a religious apologist, a social prophet, and a satirist. He was
one of the most prolific of modern authors, with over 150
titles to his name. He died in 1953, the father of five
children, and a widower for forty years.

A. N. WILSON is twice winner of the John Llewelyn
Rhys Prize (for *The Sweets of Pimlico* in 1978 and *The Laird
of Abbotsford* in 1980). His novel *The Healing Art* (1980)
won the Southern Arts Prize, the Arts Council National
Book Award, and the Somerset Maugham Award. He
lives in Oxford and is married with two children.

HILAIRE BELLOC

The Four Men

A Farrago

INTRODUCED BY
A. N. WILSON

Oxford   New York

OXFORD UNIVERSITY PRESS

1984

Oxford University Press, Walton Street, Oxford OX2 6DP

London New York Toronto
Delhi Bombay Calcutta Madras Karachi
Kuala Lumpur Singapore Hong Kong Tokyo
Nairobi Dar es Salaam Cape Town
Melbourne Auckland
and associated companies in
Beirut Berlin Ibadan Mexico City Nicosia

Oxford is a trade mark of Oxford University Press

Introduction © A. N. Wilson 1984

First published in 1911 by Thomas Nelson and Sons
First issued, with a new Introduction, as an Oxford University Press paperback 1984

British Library Cataloguing in Publication Data
Belloc, Hilaire
The four men.—(Twentieth-century classics).—(Oxford paperbacks)
I. Title
823'.912[F] PR6003.E45
ISBN 0-19-281434-6

Library of Congress Cataloging in Publication Data
Belloc, Hilaire, 1870–1953.
The four men.
I. Title.
PR6003.E45F6 1984 823'.912 83-25021
ISBN 0-19-281434-6 (pbk.)

Set by Herts Typesetting Services, Hertford
Printed in Great Britain by
Richard Clay (The Chaucer Press) Ltd.
Bungay, Suffolk

INTRODUCTION

BY A. N. WILSON

THE wisdom of Belloc can not endure, for it was too obviously right. It is only by his folly that he will be remembered. Most of his astonishingly varied and prolific output of books has been forgotten today. It is because of their truth that we cannot bear to read them. His works of political analysis—*The Servile State*, *The Party System of The House of Commons*, and *Monarchy*—are crammed with wisdom. But it is an intolerable, pessimistic wisdom; the wisdom of a man who says 'I told you so' after the horse has bolted, and who is not entirely sorry to point out that the stable door, far from being better closed, was warped and torn from its hinges years ago.

His political position was arrived at by circuitous routes. His literary antecedents in this area were Rousseau, Cobbett, and Pope Leo XIII. Of these, Cobbett was perhaps the most important, for he seemed to foresee the whole sorry history of Western 'capitalist' democracies. Belloc, very young, came to realize that he was watching the ancient civilization of Europe in its death-throes. He saw (aided largely by the *Rerum Novarum* encyclical of Leo XIII) that socialism could no more destroy the evils of capitalism than a flame-gun could put out a fire. The evils of both systems were fundamentally similar. Long before the days when Belloc was an MP for an industrial Northern constituency (1906–10) the wage slaves had been packed into city slums and had lost any chance of independence. State socialism when it came (whatever its apparent benevolence towards their physical plight) would have no desire to give them back their independence. Only by a fair distribution of property could men and women be free to lead independent lives.

Today we see all this clearly enough. A man who has his own income, his own house, his own land, and his own means of livelihood, is different in kind from the man who is dependent on a master (whether an employer or the State) dishing out benevolence. Unfortunately, although we can see it very clearly, it is too late to find a remedy. Perhaps it was already too late in Belloc's day. Few enough people took any notice of his political ideas at the time. At least we can now see that the world would be better if his creed had been operable. We would all like to be independent, with our own home and our own means of livelihood. Belloc devised a system of taxation which was really a prohibition against greed, and a declaration of a truth which has been rephrased in modern times: 'Small is beautiful.'

That is to say, a reasonably prosperous and enterprising small shopkeeper would pay almost no tax at all. Once he tried to expand and buy himself two or three shops, his tax would go up. If he attempted (an abomination never foreseen, even by Belloc) to start up a chain of supermarkets, he would, in effect, have his wealth confiscated. As it is, we have a system of taxation in which almost everyone has to give away more than a third of their income, paying for things which in a more just society we should not need. Padre Pio, the Italian saint of modern times, used to say that if the Christians were really Christian, there would be no need for Communism. That is the essence of Belloc's political creed, and it is the reason that no one listened to him. A small proportion of the world was too greedy, and the greater part was too ignorant, or too frightened, to put any of his ideas into practice.

It is easy to imagine an out-and-out capitalist and an out-and-out socialist reading Belloc today and both coming to the same scornful conclusion. Without huge injections of capital, where do you get your 'growth'? Politicians of all complexions have been yelling at us since the beginning of the century that we need 'growth': a higher standard of living, a bigger industrial output, and an anxious annual perusal of the Gross National Product. If Belloc had had his way, there would have been no 'growth' of this kind. You do not need 'growth' if all you require is a house in the country, some acreage for hay, a few cows and pigs and horses, and perhaps a boat to sail in.

'Growth' sounds like a very natural word. But on the lips of politicians it is the very enemy of nature. Their desire for 'growth' is the direct cause of the destruction and uglification of Europe, the spoiling of so much splendid architecture and the end of rural life which had gone on unchanged (in most essential features) for hundreds of years until our own century. 'Growth' has destroyed more of Europe than war. For in order to have Growth and Capitalism and Socialism, in order to keep the whole monstrous machine in operation, we needed more belchingly ugly factories, and (before the days of the 'new technology') men to work in them, with, of course, the hideous blocks and boxes in which the urban poor accommodated their families.

For the last hundred years, therefore, almost anyone who could afford to get out of our industrial towns has done so, bringing country life to an end by so doing. In the south of England in particular—the country Belloc liked best—rural villages have become little more than dormitories where refugees from the 'Servile State' can escape the modern town. With their coming, and the inevitable increase in property values, any ideal of 'peasant ownership'—of every man in Sussex having three acres and a cow—had to be discarded very quickly. In fact, the very stuff of rural life (the land) became little more than a toy. You could not afford three acres in Sussex today unless you were a stockbroker.

Belloc's prophecies are therefore melancholy and ultimately desperate. Despair is the note of much of his poetry: 'Ha'nacker's down and England's done.' He was in many ways a cynic. One of his grandchildren once witnessed him, in extreme old age, stagger drunkenly out of the Black Horse at Horsham and scatter what at first appeared to be leaves in the gutter. Then, with his old blackthorn stick, he pushed these 'leaves' along the gutter until they disappeared down the drain-hole. They were not leaves. They were a roll of pound notes. Nor was Belloc ever a rich man. This cynical, drunken gesture is all of a piece with his humour and, which is closely related, his religion. Like other 'Catholic men who live upon wine' (say, Chaucer), he felt on the one hand a *contemptus mundi*; on the other, a jolly sense that this world 'nis but a faire', a passage to a better place and a more abiding city but, because it is such a passage, a place to be infinitely valued, treasured, and enjoyed.

*

All these preoccupations lurk beneath the surface of *The Four Men*, which is subtitled 'A Farrago'—that is a hotchpotch, a jumble, or a mess. It is not a completely solemn book. Like Belloc himself it is a strange mixture of tones, of pathos and irony, of raucous hilarity and heart-broken anger. In 1901 Belloc had walked from Toul, the old garrison town where he had done his national service in the French army. It was a ramble which turned into a pilgrimage. The result of his journey was *The Path to Rome*, the book with which his name will always be associated. At first glance it seems a little like Stevenson's *Travels on a Donkey*, an ambling, chaotic, witty Victorian travelogue. But as the journey progresses we see that it is an essay on the delights of being European. It is an extraordinarily, some would say a stridently, self-confident book for a young man of 30 to have written. He is at the centre of the stage all the time talking to himself.

If *The Path to Rome* had an underlying theme, though, it could be summed up in the sailor's song from *The Four Men*:

> Oh, I thank my God for this at the least,
> I was born in the West and not in the East,
> And He made me a human instead of a beast,
>   Whose hide is covered with hair.

The Path to Rome was published in 1902, and when he got his copy of the book from the publisher Belloc began to doodle on it the opening sentences of *The Four Men*. He conceived the idea of writing a similar travel book. Only this time, instead of making a pilgrimage to the centre of European Christendom, he would journey deep into the county of Sussex where, in his early infancy, his widowed mother had made her home.

As I was sitting in the 'George' at Robertsbridge, drinking that port of theirs and staring at the fire, there arose in me a multitude of thoughts through which at last came floating a vision of the woods of home and of another place—the lake where the Arun rises.

For some reason or another, Belloc did not continue with the scheme. He rarely took long to write a book: a novel could be penned in a week; his biography of *James II* was not very unusual in being completed within ten days. But in 1902 the time was not ripe for *The Four Men* and indeed, in the nine years before it was finished, he published thirty-seven other. titles: essays, theology, travel books, novels, histories, and biographies.

In 1906 he and his wife, having led a complicated existence divided between a house in Chelsea and rented houses in Slindon near Chichester, decided to buy a house of their own in Sussex. They lighted on the old mill and village shop at Shipley near Horsham (which Belloc always pronounced Horse-hum) and they moved there with their five children in the same year.

There was not much money for 'improvements', and those which were attempted were decorative rather than practical. Lord Astor gave them a staircase from one of his houses, hugely out of scale with the rambling row of cottages which Belloc called King's Land. They nevertheless installed it, and planned to build a grand entrance hall to be worthy of it, never in the event completed. On the ground floor, incongruously, they left the shop much as it was. To this day the front room at King's Land is lined with grocers' drawers and cupboards. A dark passage leads to the dining-room, which Belloc and his friends panelled with the blackest oak. Upstairs, out of a box-room on the half landing, he and his wife constructed a chapel where, from early days, Mass was said and the Blessed Sacrament reserved. It seemed as though the lonely aspirations of his poem 'The South Country' were being put into effect:

> I never get between the pines
> But I smell the Sussex air;
> Nor I never come on a belt of sand
> But my home is there.
> And along the sky the line of the Downs
> So noble and so bare.

A lost thing could I never find
  Nor a broken thing mend:
And I fear I shall be all alone
  When I get towards the end.
Who will be there to comfort me
  Or who will be my friend?

If I ever become a rich man
  Or if ever I grow to be old,
I will build a house with deep thatch
  To shelter me from the cold,
And there shall the Sussex songs be sung
  And the story of Sussex told.

King's Land, in a bizarre sort of way, embodied this not unembarrassing ideal, even though, with its superabundance of doors and corridors, it can never have sheltered anyone very effectively from the cold. In Belloc's lifetime (he died in 1953) it never had gas or electricity. Yet it was here that his family grew up and his friends came to stay and the legend of King's Land was fostered and perpetuated. For initiates and intimates its incomparable 'atmosphere' made up for any want of physical comforts: the absence, for instance, of any very adequate bathroom. Christmas at King's Land was kept in high medieval fashion deep into Belloc's old age. J. B. Morton ('Beachcomber') has left his impressions of it:

It was the custom of the house to hear the three masses in the chapel above the dining-room, but this year Father Vincent McNabb was unable to come, so we were to go to West Grinstead for the midnight Mass. But before this there was much to be done. Soon after darkness had fallen on Christmas Eve the children of the village arrived, with their parents and relatives, and plentiful food and drink were provided for them. They were then entertained by a magic lantern, after which they were brought to the hall, where there was a tall Christmas tree, with little coloured candles and presents among its branches. Each child was given a small present, and then a sixpence. After this, they all sang songs and played games—the traditional games of this part of Sussex. When they grew tired of this, they were taken to the Crib, and gathered round it, they, their parents and the rest of us sang carols. A large jovial man with a tremendous voice led the singing and I was told that he was the miller.

When the children had gone we had a collation, and then drove to West Grinstead, with Belloc himself at the wheel of the Ford, wearing a bowler hat. As we went along the frosty lanes we sang the *Adeste fideles* in chorus . . .*

I quote this to show that the rumbustiousness of *The Four Men*, particularly of The Sailor, are direct reflections of Belloc's own personality and way of conducting himself. J. B. Morton could have been transcribing a passage of *The Four Men*, but for the presence of the motor car.

Not everyone, of course, found King's Land so sympathetic. When A. C. Benson, the diarist and author of 'Land of Hope and Glory', went there in 1911, he was horrified. The house was 'unutterably frowsy, mean, with vulgar accumulation of hideous objects, old and new . . . Belloc himself emerged from the shadows in slippers, very disshevelled, beery, smoky, un-pleasant, with shiny tail coat.' The whole atmosphere for Benson was that of 'a gypsy encampment'.†

Belloc always inspired, as these two witnesses would make clear, violently opposed reactions. He was, and is, much detested, not least among his co-religionists. When Benson visited him in 1911, eight years had passed since he had doodled the first sentence of *The Four Men*. In that time, he had hardened, and grown disillusioned. His parliamentary career, though colourful, had been unsuccessful. Perhaps if he had been rich enough, he would have tried to continue with it. But the Liberal Parliament of 1906–10 had not inspired him with any great confidence in the processes of democracy. On the one hand he was shocked by the extent to which the two major parties were governed by the *same* clique of people. The notion that Arthur Balfour was 'in Opposition' to H. H. Asquith struck Belloc as patently ludicrous. Both men belonged to the same social set, shot at the same grouse, sat at the same dinner tables, and tried to commit adultery with the same women. It was hardly a

---

* J. B. Morton: *Hilaire Belloc* (Hollis and Carter, 1955) p. 27
† David Newsome: *On the Edge of Paradise* (John Murray, 1980) p. 285

surprise to Belloc, when the great constitutional crisis blew up in
1910, that Asquith should have shown himself to be in cahoots
with the Tories and, unlike Belloc and other 'left-wingers' in the
Liberal party, to have no desire for a revolutionary shake-up in
the whole system and the abolition of the House of Peers. But at
the same time Belloc was equally shocked by the blatant corruption of the so-called radicals like Lloyd George.

Parliamentary life, as well as hardening the edge of his
cynicism, took Belloc far from home. In the summer of 1911,
when he had been gone from the House of Commons six months,
he fell to reflecting how little time he had spent at King's Land
with his family in previous years. He felt lonely and alienated.

It was then that he picked up his doodle of *The Four Men*, still
dated 29 October 1902, and added at the beginning 'Nine years
ago'.

And I said to myself inside my own mind, 'What are you doing? You are
upon some business that takes you far, not even for ambition or for
adventure, but only to earn. And you will cross the sea and earn money
and you will come back and spend more than you have earned. But all
the while your life runs past you like a river, and the things that are of
moment to men you do not heed at all.'

He could not know how true his words would prove to be, nor
how soon they would come true. He was 41 years old and he
began his 'Farrago'. 'Myself', the chief character of *The Path to
Rome*, is joined in this book by three others: a Poet, a Sailor, and a
disillusioned old man called Grizzlebeard. They are all, of
course, Belloc himself—aspects of his nature. The Four Men
ramble through Sussex, as Belloc himself so often liked to do with
his friends, in search of the Arun.

It is a hostile criticism of most books to say that they have
'dated'. But to say it of *The Four Men* is to encapsulate what is its
glory. It is like a series of happy snapshots taken at random
before a cataclysm. There will always be those who find Belloc
distasteful, just as the squeamish Arthur Benson hated the
'gypsy' atmosphere of King's Land. Certainly, Belloc struts and
poses:

> I pray good beef and I pray good beer
> This holy night of all the year,
> But I pray detestable drink to them
> That give no honour to Bethlehem.

But consider the moment towards the end of the book when they go up on the Downs above Chichester:

The air was pure and cold, as befitted All-Hallows, and the far edges of the Downs toward the Hampshire border had level lines of light above them, deeply coloured, full of departure and of rest. There was a little mist above the meadows of the Rother, and a white line of it in the growing darkness under the edges of the hills. It was not yet quite dark, but the first stars had come into the sky, and the pleasant scent of the wood fires was already strong upon the evening air when we found ourselves outside a large inn standing to the north of the road, behind a sort of green recess or common. Here were several carts standing out in the open, and a man stood with a wagon and a landaulette or two, and dogcarts as well, drawn up in the great courtyard.

This scene of the Sussex/Hampshire border before the popularity of the internal combustion engine, has a terrible poignancy for us. Belloc knew that he was immortalizing a world which was soon to vanish for ever; destroyed not by accident, but by human folly. *The Four Men* triumphs by its celebration of detail such as this, juxtaposed with its nonsense, its drunkenness, and the faintly bogus-seeming Merry-Englandism of its Catholic good cheer.

The Path to Rome had been a spiritual journey in which Belloc reaffirmed his place, and that of his readers by implication, in the great European Catholic tradition. That tradition was largely broken by the First World War. *The Four Men* makes a less certain journey, rambling like the rolling English drunkard of Chesterton's poem. He described it as a farrago, a hotchpotch, and so it is. But it is also an elegy. However much, in his own person, his own household, and his own writings, he tried to embody the ancient values, he was painfully aware that the battle would be lost. It celebrates a vanishing landscape and an obsolete life-style. Even its humour, much of it, seems pre-

Chaucerian.   But running through that humour, as through the
quest and the conversations of the Four Men themselves, there is
the reassuring sense that, though here we have no abiding city,
we journey to a place where the broken things will be mended
and the lost things found.

THE FOUR MEN

A Farrago

BY HILAIRE BELLOC

The Southern Hills and the South Sea
They blow such gladness into me,
That when I get to Burton Sands
And smell the smell of the Home Lands,
My heart is all renewed and fills
With the Southern Sea and the South Hills.

And I will sing Gol = ier!

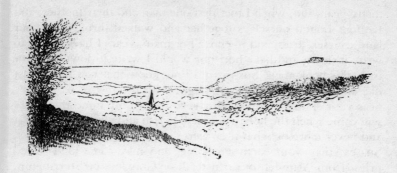

PREFACE

MY County, it has been proved in the life of every man that though his loves are human, and therefore changeable, yet in proportion as he attaches them to things unchangeable, so they mature and broaden.

On this account, Dear Sussex, are those women chiefly dear to men who, as the seasons pass, do but continue to be more and more themselves, attain balance, and abandon or forget vicissitude. And on this account, Sussex, does a man love an old house, which was his father's, and on this account does a man come to love with all his heart, that part of earth which nourished his boyhood. For it does not change, or if it changes, it changes very little, and he finds in it the character of enduring things.

In this love he remains content until, perhaps, some sort of warning reaches him, that even his own County is approaching its doom. Then, believe me, Sussex, he is anxious in a very different way; he would, if he could, preserve his land in the flesh, and keep it there as it is, forever. But since he knows he cannot do that, 'at least,' he says, 'I will keep her image, and that shall remain.' And as a man will paint with a peculiar passion a face which he is only permitted to see for a little time, so will one passionately set down one's own horizon and one's fields before they are forgotten and have become a different thing. Therefore it is that I have put down in writing what happened to me now so

many years ago, when I met first one man and then another, and
we four bound ourselves together and walked through all your
land, Sussex, from end to end. For many years I have meant to
write it down and have not; nor would I write it down now, or
issue this book at all, Sussex, did I not know that you, who must
like all created things decay, might with the rest of us be very
near your ending. For I know very well in my mind that a day
will come when the holy place shall perish and all the people of it
and never more be what they were. But before that day comes,
Sussex, may your earth cover me, and may some loud-voiced
priest from Arundel, or Grinstead, or Crawley, or Storrington,
but best of all from home, have sung Do Mi Fa Sol above my
bones.

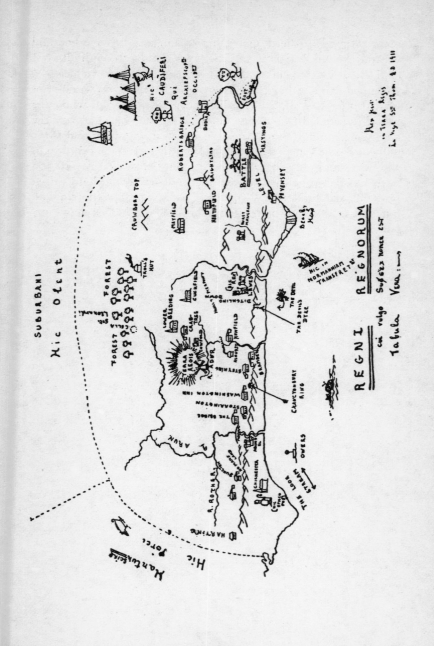

THE TWENTY-NINTH OF
OCTOBER 1902

THE TWENTY-NINTH OF OCTOBER
1902

NINE years ago, as I was sitting in the 'George' at Robertsbridge, drinking that port of theirs and staring at the fire, there arose in me a multitude of thoughts through which at last came floating a vision of the woods of home and of another place—the lake where the Arun rises.

And I said to myself, inside my own mind:

'What are you doing? You are upon some business that takes you far, not even for ambition or for adventure, but only to earn. And you will cross the sea and earn your money, and you will come back and spend more than you have earned. But all the while your life runs past you like a river, and the things that are of moment to men you do not heed at all.'

As I thought this kind of thing and still drank up that port, the woods that overhang the reaches of my river came back to me so clearly that for the sake of them, and to enjoy their beauty, I put my hand in front of my eyes, and I saw with every delicate appeal that one's own woods can offer, the steep bank over Stoke, the valley, the high ridge which hides a man from Arundel, and Arun turning and hurrying below. I smelt the tide.

Not ever, in a better time, when I had seen it of reality and before my own eyes living, had that good picture stood so plain; and even the colours of it were more vivid than they commonly are in our English air; but because it was a vision there was no sound, nor could I even hear the rustling of the leaves, though I saw the breeze gusty on the water-meadow banks, and ruffling up a force against the stream.

Then I said to myself again:

'What you are doing is not worth while, and nothing is worth while on this unhappy earth except the fulfilment of a man's desire. Consider how many years it is since you saw your home, and for how short a time, perhaps, its perfection will remain. Get up and go back to your own place if only for one day; for you have this great chance that you are already upon the soil of your own country, and that Kent is a mile or two behind.'

As I said these things to myself I felt as that man felt of whom everybody has read in Homer with an answering heart: that 'he longed as he journeyed to see once more the smoke going up from his own land, and after that to die.'

Then I hit the table there with my hand, and as though there were no duty nor no engagements in the world, and I spoke out loud (for I thought myself alone). I said:

'I will go from this place to my home.'

When I had said this the deeper voice of an older man answered:

'And since I am going to that same place, let us journey there together.'

I turned round, and I was angry, for there had been no one with me when I had entered upon this reverie, and I had thought myself alone.

I saw then, sitting beyond the table, a tall man and spare, well on in years, vigorous; his eyes were deep set in his head; they were full of travel and of sadness; his hair was of the colour of steel; it was curled and plentiful, and on his chin was a strong, full beard, as grey and stiff as the hair of his head.

'I did not know that you were here,' I said, 'nor do I know how you came in, nor who you are; but if you wish to know what it

was made me speak aloud although I thought myself alone, it was
the memory of this county, on the edge of which I happen now to
be by accident for one short hour, till a train shall take me out of
it.'

Then he answered, in the same grave way that he had spoken
before:

'For the matter of that it is my county also—and I heard you
say more than that.'

'Yes, I said more than that, and since you heard me you know
what I said. I said that all the world could be thrown over but
that I would see my own land again, and tread my own county
from here and from now, and since you have asked me what part
especially, I will tell you. My part of Sussex is all that part from
the valley of Arun, and up the Western Rother too, and so over
the steep of the Downs to the Norewood, and the lonely place
called No Man's Land.'

He said to me, nodding slowly:

'I know these also,' and then he went on. 'A man is more
himself if he is one of a number; so let us take that road together,
and, as we go, gather what company we can find.'

I was willing enough, for all companionship is good, but
chance companionship is the best of all; but I said to him, first:

'If we are to be together for three days or four (since it will take
us that at least to measure the whole length of Sussex), tell me
your name, and I will tell you mine.'

He put on the little smile which is worn by men who have
talked to very many different kinds of their fellows, and he said:

'My name is of a sort that tells very little, and if I told it it
would not be worth telling. What is your name?'

'My name,' I said to him, 'is of importance only to those who
need to know it; it might be of importance to my masters had I
such, but I have none. It is not of importance to my equals.
And since you will not tell me yours, and we must call each other
something, I shall call you Grizzlebeard, which fixes you very
well in my mind.'

'And what shall I call you,' he said, 'during so short a journey?'

'You may call me Myself,' I answered, 'for that is the name I shall give to my own person and my own soul, as you will find when I first begin speaking of them as occasion serves.'

It was agreed thus between us that we should walk through the whole county to the place we knew, and recover, while yet they could be recovered, the principal joys of the soul, and gather, if we could gather it, some further company; and it was agreed that, as our friendship was chance, so chance it should remain, and that these foolish titles should be enough for us to know each other by.

When, therefore, we had made a kind of pact (but not before) I poured out a great deal of my port for him into a silver mug which he habitually kept in his pocket, and drinking the rest from my own glass, agreed with him that we would start the next day at dawn, with our faces westward along the Brightling road—that is, up into the woods and to the high sandy land from which first, a long way off, one sees the Downs.

All this was on the evening of the 29th October in the year 1902; the air was sharp, but not frosty, and, outside, drove the last clouds of what had been for three days a great gale.

Next morning, having slept profoundly, without giving a warning to any one who had engaged us or whom we had engaged, but cutting ourselves quite apart from care and from the world, we set out with our faces westward, to reach at last the valley of the Arun and the things we knew.

THE THIRTIETH OF
OCTOBER 1902

THE THIRTIETH OF OCTOBER

1902

THERE was still wind in the sky, and clouds shaped to it, and driving before it in the cold morning as we went up the lane by Scalands Gate and between the leafless woods; and still the road rose until we came to Brightling village, and there we thought that we would step into the inn and breakfast, for we had walked four miles, and all that way up hill we had hardly said a word one to the other.

But when we were come into the inn we found there a very jovial fellow with a sort of ready smile behind his face, and eyes that were direct and keen. But these eyes of his were veiled with the salt of the sea, and paler than the eyes of a landsman would have been; for by the swing of his body as he sat there, and the ease of his limbs, he was a sailor. So much was very clear. Moreover, he had a sailor's cap on with a shiny peak, and his clothes were of the sailor's cut, and his boots were not laced but were pulled on, and showed no divisions anywhere.

As we came in we greeted this man and he us. He asked us whence we had come; we said from Robertsbridge; he told us that for his part he had slept that night in the inn, and when he

had had breakfast he was setting out again, and he asked us
whither we were going. Then I said to him:

'This older man and I have inclined ourselves to walk westward with no plan, until we come to the better parts of the
county, that is, to Arun and to the land I know.'

The Sailor. 'Why, that will suit me very well.'

Grizzlebeard. 'How do you mean that will suit you very well?'

The Sailor. 'Why, I mean that it is my intention also to walk
westward, for I have money in my pocket, and I think it will last
a few days.'

Myself. 'Doubtless you have a ship in Portsmouth or in Southampton, which, if you come with us, you will join?'

The Sailor. 'No, nor in Bosham either, of which the song says,
'Bosham that is by Selsea.' There is no little ship waiting for me
in Bosham harbour, but I shall fall upon my feet. So have I lived
since I began this sort of life, and so I mean to end it.'

Grizzlebeard. 'It will not end as you choose.'

When I had asked for breakfast for us two as well as for him, I
said to the Sailor, 'If you are to walk with us, by what name shall
we call you?'

'Why that,' said the Sailor, 'will depend upon what name you
bear yourselves.'

'Why,' said I, 'this older man here is called Grizzlebeard. It is
not his family's name, but his own, and as for myself, my name is
Myself, and a good name too—the dearest sounding name in all
the world.'

'Very well,' said the Sailor, pulling his chair up to the table and
pouring himself out a huge great bowl of tea, 'then you may call
me Sailor, which is the best name in the world, and suits me well
enough, I think, for I believe myself to be the master sailor of all
sailors, and I have sailed upon all the seas of the world.'

Grizzlebeard. 'I see that you will make a good companion.'

The Sailor. 'Yes, for as long as I choose; but you must not be
surprised if I go off by this road or by that at any hour, without
your leave or any other man's; for so long as I have money in my
pocket I am determined to see the world.'

Myself. 'We are well met, Sailor, you and Grizzlebeard and I in this parish of Brightling, which, though it lies so far from the most and the best of our county, is in a way a shrine of it.'

Grizzlebeard. 'This I never heard of Brightling, but of Hurstmonceaux.'

Myself. 'There may be shrines and shrines on any land, and sanctities of many kinds. For you will notice, Grizzlebeard, or rather you should have noticed already, having lived so long, that good things do not jostle.'

The Sailor. 'But why do you say this of Brightling? Is it perhaps because of these great folds of woods which are now open to the autumn and make a harp to catch the wind? Certainly if I'd woken here from illness or long sleep I should know by the air and by the trees in what land I was.'

Grizzlebeard. 'No, he was thinking of the obelisk which draws eyes to itself from Sussex all round.'

Myself. 'I was thinking of something far more worthy, and of the soul of a man. For do you not note the sign of this inn by which it is known?'

The Sailor. 'Why, it is called "The Fuller's Arms"; there being so many sheep I take it, and therefore so much wool and therefore fulling.'

Myself. 'No, it is not called so for such a reason, but after the arms or the name of one Fuller, a squire of these parts, who had in him the Sussex heart and blood, as had Earl Godwin and others famous in history. And indeed this man Fuller deserves to be famous and to be called, so to speak, the very demigod of my county, for he spent all his money in a roaring way, and lived in his time like an immortal being conscious of what was worth man's while during his little passage through the daylight. I have heard it said that Fuller of Brightling, being made a Knight of the Shire for the County of Sussex in the time when King George the Third was upon the throne, had himself drawn to Westminster in a noble great coach, with six huge, hefty, and determined horses to draw it, but these were not of the Sussex breed, for there is none. And he——'

Grizzlebeard. 'You say right that they were not "Sussex horses," for there are only two things in Sussex which Sussex deigns to give its name to, and the first is the spaniel, and the second is the sheep. Note you, many kingdoms and counties and lands are prodigal of their names, because their names are of little account and in no way sacred, so that one will give its name to a cheese and another to a horse, and another to some kind of iron-work or other, and another to clotted cream or to butter, and another to something ridiculous, as to a cat with no tail. But it is not so with Sussex, for our name is not a name to be used like a label and tied on to common things, seeing that we were the first place to be created when the world was made, and we shall certainly be the last to remain, regal and at ease when all the rest is very miserably perishing on the Day of Judgment by a horrible great rain of fire from Heaven. Which will fall, if I am not mis-taken, upon the whole earth, and strike all round the edges of the county, consuming Tonbridge, and Appledore (but not Rye), and Horley, and Ockley, and Hazelmere, and very certainly Petersfield and Havant, and there shall be an especial woe for Hayling Island; but not one hair of the head of Sussex shall be singed, it has been so ordained from the beginning, and that in spite of Burwash and those who dwell therein.'

Myself. 'Now you have stopped me in the midst of what I was saying about Fuller, that noble great man sprung from this noble great land.'

The Sailor. 'You left him going up to Westminster in a coach with six great horses, to sit in Parliament and be a Knight of the Shire.'

Myself. 'That is so, and, God willing, as he went he sang the song 'Golier! Golier!' and I make little doubt that until he came to the Marches of the county, and entered the barbarous places outside, great crowds gathered at his passage and cheered him as such a man should be cheered, for he was a most noble man, and very free with all good things. Nor did he know what lay before him, having knowledge of nothing so evil as Westminster, nor of anything so stuffy or so vile as her most detestable Commons House, where men sit palsied and glower, hating each other and themselves: but he knew nothing yet except broad Sussex.

'Well, then, when he had come to Westminster, very soon

there was a day in which the Big-wigs would have a debate, all empty and worthless, upon Hot Air, or the value of nothingness; and the man who took most money there out of the taxes, and his first cousin who sat opposite and to whom he had promised the next wad of public wealth, and his brother-in-law and his parasite and all the rest of the thieves had begun their pompous folly, when great Fuller arose in his place, full of the South, and said that he had not come to the Commons House to talk any such balderdash, or to hear it, but contrariwise proposed, then and there, to give them an Eulogy upon the County of Sussex, from which he had come and which was the captain ground and head county of the whole world.

'This Eulogy he very promptly and powerfully began, using his voice as a healthy man should, who will drown all opposition and who can call a dog to heel from half a mile away. And indeed though a storm rose round him from all those lesser men, who had come to Westminster, not for the praise or honour of their land, but to fill their pockets, he very manfully shouted, and was heard above it all, so that the Sergeant-at-Arms grew sick with fear, and the Clerk at the Table wished he had never been born. But the Speaker, whose business it is to keep the place inane (I do not remember his name, for such men are not famous after death), stood up in his gown and called to Fuller that he was out of order. And since Fuller would not yield, every man in the House called out "Order!" eight or nine hundred times. But when they were exhausted, the great Fuller, Fuller of Brightling, cried out over them all:

'"Do you think I care for you, you insignificant little man in the wig? Take that!" And with these words he snapped his fingers in the face of the bunch of them, and walked out of the Commons House, and got into his great coach with its six powerful horses, and ordering their heads to be set southwards he at last regained his own land, where he was received as such a man should be, with bells ringing and guns firing, little boys cheering, and all ducks, hens, and pigs flying from before his approach to the left and to the right of the road. Ever since that day it has been held a singular honour and one surpassing all others to be a squire of Brightling, but no honour whatsoever to be a member of the Commons House. He spent all his great fortune upon the poor of Sussex and of his own parish, bidding them drink deep and eat hearty as being habits the best preservative of life, until at last he also died. There is the story of Fuller of Brightling, and may we all deserve as well as he.'

The Sailor. 'The great length of your story, Myself, has enabled me to make a very excellent breakfast, for which I shall pay, bidding you and Grizzlebeard pay each for your own, as is the custom of the parish where I was born, and one I hope you will admire while I still have cash, but forget when I have spent it. And if in talking so much you have eaten little, I cannot help it, but I must take the road.'

So saying the Sailor rose up and wiped his lips very carefully with his napkin, and put down a sum of money upon which he had agreed with the landlord, and we also paid for ourselves, and then we all three set out under the high morning for Heathfield, and were ready to talk of Jack Cade (who very nearly did for the rich, but who most unfortunately came by a knock on the head in these parts), when we perceived upon the road before us a lanky fellow, moving along in a manner quite particular to men of one sort throughout the world, men whose thoughts are always wool-gathering, and who seem to have no purpose, and yet in some way are by the charity of their fellows kept fed and clothed.

'Mark you that man,' said Grizzlebeard, 'for I think we can make him of our company, and if I am not mistaken he shall add to it what you (speaking to the Sailor) and Myself there, and I also lack. For this morning has proved us all three to be cautious folk, men of close speech and affectation, knaves knowing well our way about the world, and careful not to give away so much as our own names: skinflints paying each his own shot, and in many other ways fellows devoted to the Devil. But this man before us, if I mistake not, is of a kind much nearer God.'

As Grizzlebeard said this, we watched the man before us more closely, and we saw that as he walked his long limbs seemed to have loose joints, his arms dangled rather than swang, he steered

no very straight course along the road, and under his felt hat with
its narrow brim there hung tawny hair much too long, and in
no way vigorous. His shirt was soft, grey and dirty, and of
wool, and his collar made one with it, the roll of which just
peeped above his throat, and his coat was of velveteen, like a
keeper's, but he was not like a keeper in any other way, and no
one would have trusted him with a gun.

'Who knows but this thing may be an artist?' said the Sailor in
an awed voice to me, as we came nearer.

Myself. 'I do not think so. An artist would not be so
nonchalant. Even in youth their debts oppress them, and they
make certain fixed and firm gestures, for they are men that work
with their hands. But this thing is loose hung, and though I will
make certain he has debts, I will be certain also that he cares
nothing for them, and could not tell you their amount to within
half of the true total.'

By this time, since we walked steadily, and he shambling, as I
have said, we had nearly come up with him, and we heard him
crooning to himself in a way that might have irritated any weary
listener, for the notes of his humming were not distinct at all, and
he seemed to care little where the tune began or ended. Then we
saw him stop suddenly, pull a pencil out of some pocket or other,
and feel about in several more for paper as we supposed.

'I am right,' said Grizzlebeard in triumph. 'He is a Poet!'

Hearing our voices for the first time the youth turned slowly
round, and when we saw his eyes we knew indeed that
Grizzlebeard was right. His eyes were arched and large as
though in a perpetual surprise, and they were of a warm grey
colour. They did not seem to see the things before them, but
other things beyond; and while the rest of his expression changed
a little to greet us, his eyes did not change. Moreover they
seemed continually sad.

Before any of us could address this young man, he asked
suddenly for a knife.

'Do you think it safe to let him have one?' said the Sailor to me.

'It is to sharpen this pencil with,' said the stranger, putting
forth a stub of an H.B. much shorter than his thumb. He held it

forward rather pitifully and uncertainly, with its blunt, broken point upwards.

'You had better take this,' said Grizzlebeard, handing him a pencil in better condition. 'Have you no knife of your own?'

'I have lost it,' said the other sadly. His voice was mournful as he said it, so I suppose it had been his friend.

Grizzlebeard. 'Well, take mine and write down quickly what you had to write, for such things I know by my own experience to be fugitive.'

The stranger looked at him a moment and then said:

'I have forgotten what I was going to say . . . I mean, to write.'

The Sailor (*with a groan*). 'He has forgotten his own name!' (*Then more loudly*), 'Poet! Let us call you Poet, and come your way with us. We will look after you, and in return you shall write us verse: bad verse, oughly verse into which a man may get his teeth. Not sloppy verse, not wasty, pappy verse; not verse blanchified, but strong, heavy, brown, bad verse; made up and knotty; twisted verse of the fools. Such verse as versifiers write when they are moved to versifying by the deeper passions of other men, having themselves no facilities with the Muse.'

The Poet. 'I do not understand you.'

But Grizzlebeard took his arm affectionately, as though he were his father, and said, 'Come, these men are good-natured enough, but they have just had breakfast, and it is not noon, so they are in a hunting mood, and for lack of quarry hunt you. But you shall not reply to them. Only come westward with us and be our companion until we get to the place where the sun goes down, and discover what makes it so glorious.'

On hearing this the Poet was very pleased. He had long desired to find that place, and said that he had been walking towards it all his life. But he confessed to us a little shamefacedly that he had no money, except three shillings and a French penny, which last some one had given him out of charity, taking him for a beggar a little way out of Brightling that very day.

'If, however,' he said, 'you are prepared to pay for me in all things no matter what I eat or drink or read or in any other way disport myself, why, I shall be very glad to drive that bargain with you.'

Myself. 'Poet! That shall be understood between us! And you shall order what you will. You shall not feel constrained. It is in the essence of good fellowship that the poor man should call for the wine, and the rich man should pay for it.'

'I am not a poor man,' said the Poet in answer to me gently, 'only I have forgotten where I left my money. I know I had three pounds yesterday, but I think I paid a sovereign for a shilling beyond Brede, and in Battle (it must have been) I forgot to pick up my change. As for the third pound it may turn up, but I have looked for it several times this morning, and I am beginning to fear that it is gone . . . Now I remember it!'

The Sailor. 'What? More luck? Be certain of this much! We will not turn backwards for your one pound or for five of them.'

The Poet. 'No, not that. When I said "I remember," I meant something else. I meant the line I had in my head as you came along and changed my thoughts.'

The Sailor. 'I do not want to hear it.'

The Poet. 'It was,

> I wonder if these little pointed hills . . .'

Grizzlebeard. 'Yes, and what afterwards?'

The Poet (*a little pained*). 'Nothing, I am afraid.' He waved his hands limply towards the north. 'But you will perceive that the little hills are pointed hereabouts.'

The Sailor. 'I never yet thanked my parents for anything in my life, but now I thank them for that which hitherto has most distressed me, that they set me to the hard calling of the sea. For if I had not been apprenticed, Bristol fashion, when I was a child to a surly beast from Holderness, I might have been a Poet, by the wrath of God.'

Grizzlebeard. 'Do not listen to him, Poet, but see! We have come into Heathfield. I think it is time either to eat or drink or do both, and to consider our companionship joined, and the first stage of our journey toward the West accomplished.'

Now in those days Heathfield was a good place for men, and will be again, for this land of Sussex orders all things towards itself, and will never long permit any degradation.

So we sat down outside the village at the edge of a little copse, which was part of a rich man's park, and we looked northward to the hill of Mayfield, where St. Dunstan pulled the Devil by the nose; and they keep the tongs wherewith he did it in Mayfield to this day.

Now as the story of the way St. Dunstan pulled the Devil by the nose has, in the long process of a thousand years, grown corrupt, distorted, and very unworthily changed from its true original, and as it is a matter which every child should know and every grown man remember for the glory of religion and to the honour of this ancient land, I will set it down here before I forget it, and you shall read it or no, precisely as you choose.

St. Dunstan, then, who was a Sussex man (for he was born a little this side of Ardingly, whatever false chroniclers may say against it, and was the son of Mr. Dunstan of the Leas, a very honest man), St. Dunstan, I say, having taken orders, which was his own look-out, and no business of ours, very rapidly rose from sub-deacon to deacon, and from deacon to priest, and from priest to bishop, and would very certainly have risen to be pope in due time, had he not wisely preferred to live in this dear county of his instead of wasting himself on foreigners.

Of the many things he did I have no space to tell you (and as it is, my story is getting longer than I like—but no matter), but one chief thing he did, memorable beyond all others. Yes, more memorable even than the miracle whereby he caused a number of laymen to fall, to his vast amusement but to their discomfiture, through the rotten flooring of a barn. And this memorable thing was his pulling of the Devil by the nose.

For you must know that the Devil, desiring to do some hurt to the people of Sussex, went about asking first one man, then another, who had the right of choice in it, and every one told him St. Dunstan. For he was their protector, as they knew, and that was why they sent the Devil to him, knowing very well that he would get the better of the Fiend, whom the men of Sussex properly defy and harass from that day to this, as you shall often find in the pages of this book.

So the Devil went up into the Weald of a May morning when everything was pleasant to the eye and to the ear, and he found

St. Dunstan sitting in Cuckfield at a table in the open air, and writing verse in Latin, which he very well knew how to do. Then said the Devil to St. Dunstan: 'I have come to give you your choice how Sussex shall be destroyed, for you must know that I have the power and the patent to do this thing, and there is no gainsaying me, only it is granted to your people to know the way by which they should perish.'

And indeed this is the Devil's way, always to pretend that he is the master, though he very well knows in his black heart that he is nothing of the kind.

Now St. Dunstan was not the fool he looked, in spite of his round face, and round tonsure, and round eyes, and he would have his sport with the Devil before he had done with him, so he answered civilly enough:

'Why, Devil, I think if we must all pass, it would be pleasanter to die by way of seawater than any other, for out of the sea came our land, and so into the sea should it go again. Only I doubt your power to do it, for we are defended against the sea by these great hills called The Downs, which will take a woundy lot of cutting through.'

'Pooh! bah!' said the Devil, rudely, in answer. 'You do not know your man! I will cut through those little things in a night and not feel it, seeing I am the father of contractors and the original master of overseers and undertakers of great works: it is child's-play to me. It is a flea-bite, a summer night's business between sunset and dawn.'

'Why, then,' said St. Dunstan, 'here is the sun nearly set over Black Down, westward of us, so go to your work; but if you have not done it by the time the cock crows over the Weald, you shall depart in God's name.'

Then the Devil, full of joy at having cheated St. Dunstan, as he thought, and at being thus able to ruin our land, which, if ever he could accomplish it, would involve the total destruction and effacement of the whole world, flew off through the air southwards, flapping his great wings. So that all the people of the Weald thought it was an aeroplane, of which instrument they are delighted observers; and many came out to watch him as he flew, and some were ready to tell others what kind of aeroplane he was, and such like falsehoods.

But no sooner was it dark than the Devil, getting a great spade sent him from his farm, set to work very manfully and strongly, digging up the Downs from the seaward side. And the sods flew and the great lumps of chalk he shovelled out left and right, so that it was a sight to see; and these falling all over the place, from the strong throwing of his spade, tumbled some of them upon Mount Caburn, and some of them upon Rackham Hill, and some here and some there, but most of them upon Cissbury, and that is how those great mounds grew up, of which the learned talk so glibly, although they know nothing of the matter whatsoever.

The Devil dug and the Devil heaved until it struck midnight in Shoreham Church, and one o'clock and two o'clock again. And as he dug his great dyke drove deeper and deeper into the Downs, so that it was very near coming out on the Wealden side, and there were not more than two dozen spits to dig before the sea would come through and drown us all.

But St. Dunstan (who knew all this), offering up the prayer, *Populus Tuus Domine* (which is the prayer of Nov. 8, Pp. alba 42, Double or quits), by the power of this prayer caused at that instant all the cocks that are in the Weald between the Western and the Eastern Rother, and from Ashdown right away to Harting Hill, and from Bodiam to Shillinglee, to wake up suddenly in defence of the good Christian people, and to haul those silly red-topped heads of theirs from under their left wings, and very broadly to crow altogether in chorus, so that such a noise was never heard before, nor will be heard thence afterwards forever; and you would have thought it was a Christmas night instead of the turn of a May morning.

The Devil, then, hearing this terrible great challenge of crowing from some million throats for seventy miles one way and twenty miles the other, stopped his digging in bewilderment, and striking his spade into the ground he hopped up on to the crest of the hill and looked in wonderment up the sky and down the sky over all the stars, wondering how it could be so near day. But in this foolish action he lost the time he needed. For even as he discovered what a cheat had been played upon him, over away beyond Hawkhurst Ridge day dawned—and with a great howl the Devil was aware that his wager was lost.

But he was firm on his right (for he loves strict dealing in oppression) and he flew away over the air this way and that, to find St. Dunstan, whom he came upon at last, not in Cuckfield but in Mayfield. Though how the Holy Man got there in so short a time I cannot tell. It is a mystery worthy of a great saint.

Anyhow, when the Devil got to Mayfield he asked where St. Dunstan was, and they told him he was saying Mass. So the Devil had to wait, pawing and chawing and whisking his tail, until St. Dunstan would come out, which he did very leisurely and smiling, and asked the Devil how the devil he did, and why it was he had not finished that task of his. But the Devil, cutting him short, said:

'I will have no monkishness, but my due!'

'Why, how is that?' said St. Dunstan in a pleased surprise.

Then the Devil told him how the cocks had all begun crowing half-an-hour before the right time, and had unjustly deprived him of his reward. For the dyke (he said) was all but finished, and now stood there nearly through the Downs. And how it was a burning shame that such a trick should have been played, and how he verily believed there had been sharp practice in the matter, but how, notwithstanding, he would have his rights, for the law was on his side.

Then St. Dunstan, scratching his chin with the forefinger of his left hand (which he was the better able to do, because he had not shaved that morning), said to the Devil in answer:

'I perceive that there is here matter for argument. But do not let us debate it here. Come rather into my little workshop in the palace yonder, where I keep all my arguments, and there I will listen to you as your case deserves.'

So, they went together towards the little workshop, St. Dunstan blithely as befits a holy man, but the Devil very grumpily and sourly. And there St. Dunstan gave the Devil a chair, and bade him talk away and present his case, while he himself would pass the time away at little tricks of smithying and ornamentary, which were his delight. And so saying, St. Dunstan blew the bellows and heated the fire of his forge, and put his enamelling tongs therein, and listened while the Devil put before him his case, with arguments so cogent, precedents so numerous, statutes so clear, and order so lucid, as never yet were heard in any court, and would have made a lawyer dance for joy. And all the while St. Dunstan kept nodding gravely and saying:

'Yes! Yes! Proceed! . . . But I have an argument against all of this!' Until at last the Devil, stung by so simple a reply repeated, said:

'Why, then, let us see your argument! For there is no argument or plea known or possible which can defeat my claim, or make me abandon it or compromise it in ever so little.'

But just as he said this St. Dunstan, pulling his tongs all hot from the forge fire, cried very suddenly and loudly:

'Here is my argument!' And with that he clapped the pincers sharply upon the Devil's nose, so that he danced and howled and began to curse in a very abominable fashion.

'Come, now!' said St. Dunstan. 'Come! This yowling is no pleading, but blank ribaldry! Will you not admit this argument of mine, and so withdraw from this Court non-suited?'

And as he said this he pulled the Devil briskly round and round the room, making him hop over tables and leap over chairs like a mountebank, and cursing the while with no set order of *demurrer*, *replevin*, *quo warranto*, *nisi prius*, *habeas corpus*, and the rest, but in good round German, which is his native speech, and all the while St. Dunstan said:

'Argue, brother! Argue, learned counsel! Plead! All this is not to the issue before the Court! Let it be yes or no! We must have particulars!' And as he thus harangued the Devil in legal fashion, he still pulled him merrily round and round the room, taking full sport of him, until, at last, the Devil could stand no more, and so, when St. Dunstan unclappered his clippers, flew instantly away.

And that is why the Devil does to this day feel so extraordinarily tender upon the subject of his nose; and in proof of the whole story (if proof were needed of a matter which is in the

Bollandists, and amply admitted of the Curia, the Propaganda, and whatever else you will), in proof of the whole story I say you have: *Imprimis*, the Dyke itself, which is still called the Devil's Dyke, and which still stands there very neatly dug, almost to the crossing of the hills. *Secundo, et valde fortior*, in Mayfield, for any one to handle and to see, the very tongs wherewith the thing was done.

And if you find the story long be certain that the Devil found it longer, for there is no tale in the world that can bore a man as fiercely as can hot iron. So back to Heathfield.

*

Well, as we sat there in Heathfield, we debated between ourselves by which way we should go westward, for all this part of The County is a Jumbled Land.

First, as in duty bound, we asked the Poet, because he was the last comer; and we found that he could not make up his mind, and when we pressed him we found further that he did not know at all by what way a man might go west from these woods. But when he heard that if any one should go through Burgess Hill and Hayward's Heath he would be going through towns of the London sort, the Poet said that rather than do that he would leave our company. For he said that in such towns the more one worked the less one had, and that yet, if one did not work at all, one died. So all he had to say upon the matter was that whether we avoided such places by the north or by the south, it was all one to him; but avoid them one way or another we must if we wished him to keep along with us.

When the Poet had thus given his opinion, Grizzlebeard and I next put the question to the Sailor, who frowned and looked very wise for a little time, and then, taking out his pencil, asked the Poet to say again exactly what his objection was; which, as the Poet gave it him, he carefully wrote down on a piece of paper. And when he had done that, he very thoughtfully filled his pipe with tobacco, rolled the paper into a spill, set fire to it, and with it lit his pipe. When he had done all these things, he said he did not care how we went, so only that we got through the bad part quickly.

He thought we might do it in the darkness. But I told him that the places would be full of policemen, who were paid to throw poor and wandering men into prison, especially by night. So he gave up the whole business.

Then Grizzlebeard and I discussed how the thing should be done, and we decided that there was nothing for it but to go by the little lanes to Irkfield, particularly remembering 'The Black Boy' where these little lanes began, and then, not sleeping at Irkfield, to go on through the darkness to Fletching, and so by more little lanes to Ardingly. In this way we who knew the county could be rid of the invaders, and creep round them to the north until we found ourselves in the forest.

Having thus decided, we set out along that road in silence, but first we bought cold meat and bread to eat upon our way, and when we came to Irkfield it was evening.

The wind had fallen. We had gone many miles that day. We were fatigued; and nothing but the fear of what lay before us prevented our sleeping in the place. For we feared that if we slept there we should next day shirk the length of the detour, and see those horrible places after all. But the Sailor asked suddenly what money there was between us. He himself, he said, had more than one pound, and he put down on the table of the inn we halted in, a sovereign and some shillings. I said that I had more than five, which was true, but I would not show it. Grizzlebeard said that what money he had was the business of no one but himself. The Poet felt in many pockets, and made up very much less than half-a-crown.

Not until all this had been done did the Sailor tell us that he had hired in that same house a little two-wheeled cart, with a strong horse and a driver, and that, for a very large sum, we might be driven all those miles through the night to Ardingly, and to the edge of the high woods, and that for his part we might come with him or not, but he would certainly drive fast through the darkness, and not sleep until he was on the forest ridge, and out of all this detestable part of the county, which was not made for men, but rather for tourists or foreigners, or London people that had lost their way.

So we climbed into his cart, and we were driven through the night by cross roads, passing no village except Fletching, until, quite at midnight, we were on the edge of the high woods, and there the driver was paid so much that he could put up and pass the night, but for our part we went on into the trees, led by the Sailor, who said he knew more of these woods than any other man.

Therefore we followed him patiently, though how he should know these woods or when he had first come upon them he would not tell.

We went through the dark trees by a long green ride, climbing the gate that a rich man had put up and locked, and passing deeper and deeper into the wild, and in the little that we said to each other, Grizzlebeard, the Sailor and I, we hoped for rest very soon; but the Sailor went on before, knowing his way like a hound, and turning down this path and that until we came suddenly to a blot in the darkness, and a square of black stretching across the trees from side to side. It was a little hut.

The Sailor first tried the door, then, finding it locked, he pulled a key from his pocket and entered, and when he had got inside out of the breeze, he struck a match and lit a candle that was there, standing on a copper stick, and we all came in and looked around.

It was one room, and a small one, of weather boarding on all the four sides. There were two small windows, which were black in the candle light, and on the side to the right of the door a great fireplace of brick, with ashes in it and small wood and logs laid, and near this fireplace was a benched ingle-nook, and there were two rugs there. But for these things there was nothing in the hut whatsoever, no book or furniture at all, except the candle-stick, and the floor was of beaten earth.

'Sailor,' said I, 'how did you come to have the key of this place?'

It was wonderful enough that he should have known his way to it. But the Sailor said:

'Why not?' and after that would tell us no more. Only he said before we slept, late as it was, we would do well to light the fire, and put upon it two or three more of the great logs that stood by, since, in the autumn cold, we none of us should sleep however much we wrapped our cloaks about our feet, unless we had our feet to a blaze. And in this he was quite right, for no matter what the weather, and even out in the open, men can always sleep if they have a fire. So we made an agreement between us that Grizzlebeard, being an old man, was to have the bench and the rugs, but that we three were to stretch ourselves before the fire, when it should be lit; and, talking so and still wide-awake, we struck matches and tried to coax the flame.

But at first, on account of the wind without, it lit badly, and the small wood was damp and smoked, and the smoke blew into our faces and into the room; and the Sailor, shielding it with his coat and trying to get a draught in that great chimney-place, said that a smoking chimney was a cursed thing.

'It is the worst thing in the world,' said the Poet peevishly; to which the Sailor answered:

'Nonsense! Death is the worst thing in the world.'

But Grizzlebeard, from where he lay on the broad bench with rugs about him, and his head resting on his hand, denied this too, speaking in a deep voice with wisdom. 'You are neither of you right,' he said. 'The worst thing in the world is the passing of human affection. No man who has lost a friend need fear death,' he said.

The Sailor. 'All that is Greek to me. If any man has made friends and lost them, it is I. I lost a friend in Lima once, but he turned up again at Valparaiso, and I can assure you that the time in between was no tragedy.'

Grizzlebeard (*solemnly*). 'You talk lightly as though you were a younger man than you are. The thing of which I am speaking is the gradual weakening, and at last the severance, of human bonds. It has been said that no man can see God and live. Here is another saying for you, very near the same: No man can be alone and live. None, not even in old age.'

He stopped and looked for some little time into the rising fire. Outside the wind went round the house, and one could hear the boughs in the darkness.

Then Grizzlebeard went on:

'When friendship disappears then there is a space left open to that awful loneliness of the outside which is like the cold of space between the planets. It is an air in which men perish utterly. Absolute dereliction is the death of the soul; and the end of living is a great love abandoned.'

Myself. 'But the place heals, Grizzlebeard.'

Grizzlebeard (*still more solemnly*). 'All wounds heal in those who are condemned to live, but in the very process of healing they harden and forbid renewal. The thing is over and done.'

He went on monotonous and grave. He said that 'everything else that there is in the action of the mind save loving is of its nature a growth: it goes through its phases of seed, of miraculous sprouting, of maturity, of somnolescence, and of decline. But with loving it is not so; for the comprehension by one soul of another is something borrowed from whatever lies outside time: it is not under the conditions of time. Then if it passes, it is past—it never grows again; and we lose it as men lose a diamond, or as men lose their honour.'

Myself. 'Since you talk of honour, Grizzlebeard, I should have thought that the loss of honour was worse than the loss of friends.'

Grizzlebeard. 'Oh, no. For the one is a positive loss, the other imaginary. Moreover, men that lose their honour have their way out by any one of the avenues of death. Not so men who lose the affection of a creature's eyes. Therein for them, I mean in death, is no solution: to escape from life is no escape from that loss. Nor of the many who have sought in death relief from their affairs is there one (at least of those I can remember) who sought that relief on account of the loss of a human heart.'

The Poet. 'When I said "it" was the worst thing in the world just now so angrily, I was foolish. I should have remembered the toothache.'

The Sailor (*eagerly and contemptuously*). 'Then there you are utterly wrong, for the earache is much worse.'

The Poet. 'I never had the earache.'

The Sailor (*still contemptuously*). 'I thought not! If you had you

would write better verse. It is your innocence of the great
emotions that makes your verse so dreadful—in the minor sense
of that word.'

Grizzlebeard. 'You are both of you talking like children. The
passing of human affection is the worst thing in the world.
When our friends die they go from us, but it is not of their own
will; or if it is of their own will, it is not of their own will in any
contradiction to ours; or even if it be of their own will in contradiction to ours and the end of a quarrel, yet it is a violent thing
and still savours of affection. But that decay of what is living in
the heart, and that numbness supervening, and that last indif-
ference—oh! these are not to be compared for unhappiness with
any other ill on this unhappy earth. And all day long and in
every place, if you could survey the world from a height and look
down into the hearts of men, you would see that frost stealing
on.'

Myself. 'Is this a thing that happens, Grizzlebeard, more
notably to the old?'

Grizzlebeard. 'No. The old are used to it. They know it, but
it is not notable to them. It is notable on the approach of middle
age. When the enthusiasms of youth have grown either stale or
divergent, and when, in the infinite opportunities which time
affords, there has been opportunity for difference between friend
and friend, then does the evil appear. The early years of a man's
life do not commonly breed this accident. So convinced are we
then, and of such energy in the pursuit of our goal, that if we
must separate we part briskly, each certain that the other is guilty
of a great wrong. The one man will have it that some criminal is
innocent, the other that an innocent man was falsely called a
criminal. The one man loves a war, the other thinks it unjust
and hates it (for all save the money-dealers think of war in terms
of justice). Or the one man hits the other in the face. These are
violent things. But it is when youth has ripened, and when the
slow processes of life begin that the danger or the certitude of this
dreadful thing appears: I mean of the passing of affection. For
the mind has settled as the waters of a lake settle in the hills; it is
full of its own convictions, it is secure in its philosophy; it will

not mould or adapt itself to the changes of another. And, therefore, unless communion be closely maintained, affection decays.
Now when it has decayed, and when at last it has altogether
passed, then comes that awful vision of which I have spoken,
which is the worst thing in the world.'

The Poet. 'The great poets, Grizzlebeard, never would admit
this thing. They have never sung or deplored the passage of
human affection; they have sung of love turned to hatred, and of
passion and of rage, and of the calm that succeeds passion, and of
the doubt of the soul and of doom, and continually they have
sung of death, but never of the evil of which you speak.'

The Sailor. 'That was because the evil was too dull; as I
confess I find it! Anything duller than the loss of a friend!
Why, it is like writing a poem on boredom or like singing a song
about Welbeck Street, to try and poetise such things! Turn
rather to this fire, which is beginning to blaze, thank God! turn
to it, and expect the morning.'

Myself. 'You Poet and you Sailor, you are both of you wrong
there. The thing has been touched upon, though very charily,
for it is not matter for art. It just skims the surface of the return
of Odysseus, and the poet Shakespeare has a song about it which
you have doubtless heard. It is sung by gentlemen painted with
grease paint and dressed in green cloth, one of whom is a Duke,
and therefore wears a feather in his cap. They sit under canvas
trees, also painted, and drink out of cardboard goblets, quite
empty of all wine; these goblets are evidently empty, for they
hold them anyhow; if there were real wine in them it would drop
out. And thus accoutred and under circumstances so ridiculous,
they sing a song called "Blow, blow, thou winter wind." Moreover, a poet has written of the evil thing in this very County of
Sussex, in these two lines:

> The things I loved have all grown wearisome,
> The things that loved me are estranged or dead.

Grizzlebeard. '"Estranged" is the word: I was looking for that
word. Estrangement is the saddest thing in the world.'

The Sailor. 'I cannot make head or tail of all this.'

The Poet. 'Have you never lost a friend?'

The Sailor. 'Dozens—as I've already told you. And the one I most regret was a doctor man whom the owners shipped with us for a run to the Plate and back again. But I have never let it weigh upon my mind.'

Grizzlebeard. 'The reason that the great poets have touched so little upon this thing is precisely because it is the worst thing in the world. It is a spur to no good deed, nor to any strong thinking, nor does it in any way emend the mind. Now the true poets, whether they will or no, are bound to emend the mind; they are constrained to concern themselves with noble things. But in this there is nothing noble. It has not even horror nor doom to enhance it; it is an end, and it is an end without fruition. It is an end which leaves no questions and no quest. It is an end without adventure, an end complete, a nothingness; and there is no matter for art in the mortal hunger of the soul.'

And after this sad speech of his we were again silent, lying now at length before the fire, and the Sailor having lit a pipe and smoking it.

Then I remembered a thing I had read once, and I said:

Myself. 'I read once in a book of a man who was crossing a heath in a wild country not far from the noise of the sea. The wind and the rain beat upon him, and it was very cold, so he was glad to see a light upon the heath a long way off. He made towards it and, coming into that place, found it to be a chapel where some twenty or thirty were singing, and there was a priest at the altar saying Mass at midnight, and there was a monk serving his Mass. Now this traveller noticed how warm and brilliant was the place; the windows shone with their colours, and all the stone was carved; the altar was all alight, and the place was full of singing, for the twenty or thirty still sang, and he sang with them . . . But their faces he could not see, for the priest who said the Mass and the man who served the Mass both had their faces from him, and all in that congregation were hooded, and their faces were turned away from him also, but their singing was loud, and he joined in it. He thought he was in fairyland. And so he was. For as that Mass ended he fell asleep, suffused with warmth, and his ears still full of music; but when he woke he found that the place was a ruin, the windows empty, and the wind roaring through; no glass, or rather a few broken panes, and these quite plain and colourless; dead leaves of trees blown in upon the altar steps, and over the whole of it the thin and miserable light of a winter dawn.

'This story which I read went on to say that the man went on his journey under that new and unhappy light of a stormy winter dawn, on over the heath in the wild country. But though he had made just such a journey the day before, yet his mind was changed. In the interlude he had lost something great; therefore the world was worth much less to him than it had been the day before, though if he had heard no singing in between, nor had seen no lights at evening, the journey would have seemed the same. This advantage first, and then that loss succeeding, had utterly impoverished him, and his journey meant nothing to him any more. This is the story which I read, and I take it you mean something of the kind.'

'Yes, I meant something of the kind,' said Grizzlebeard in answer, sighing. 'I was thinking of the light that shines through the horn, and how when the light is extinguished the horn thickens cold and dull. I was thinking of irrevocable things.'

At this the Poet, whom he had thought dozing, started to his feet.

'Oh, let us leave so disheartening a matter,' said he, 'and consider rather what is the best thing in the world than what is the worst. For in the midst of this wood, where everything is happy except man, and where the night should teach us quiet, we ought to learn or discover what is the best thing in the world.'

'I know of no way of doing that,' said the Sailor, 'but by watching the actions of men and seeing to what it is they will chiefly attach themselves. For man knows his own nature, and that which he pursues must surely be his satisfaction? Judging by which measure I determine that the best thing in the world is flying at full speed from pursuit, and keeping up hammer and thud and gasp and bleeding till the knees fail and the head grows dizzy, and at last we all fall down and that thing (whatever it is) which pursues us catches us up and eats our carcasses. This way of managing our lives, I think, must be the best thing in the world —for nearly all men choose to live thus.'

Myself. 'What you say there, Sailor, seems sound enough, but I am a little puzzled in this point: why, if most men follow their satisfaction, most men come to so wretched an end?'

The Sailor. 'Why that I cannot tell. That is their business. But certainly as I have watched men it seems to me that they regard being hunted as the best thing in the world. For one man having as much as would enable him (if he were so inclined) to see the world of God, and to eat all kinds of fruit and flesh, and to drink the best of beer, will none the less start a race with a Money-Devil: a fleet, strong Money-Devil with a goad. And when this Money-Devil has given him some five years start, say until he is nearly thirty years of age, then will that man start racing and careering and bounding and flying with the Money-Devil after him, over hill and valley, field and fen, and wood and waste, and the high heaths and the wolds, until at last (somewhere about sixty as a rule or a little later) he gives a great cry and throws up his hands and falls down. Then does the Money-Devil come and eat him up. Many millions love such a course.

'And there is also that other sort of hunt, in which some appetite or lust sets out a-chasing the jolly human, and puts him at fence and hedge, and gate and dyke, and round the spinney and over the stubble and racing over the bridge, and then double again through copse and close, and thicket and thorn, until he has spent his breath upon the high Downs, and then, after a little respite, a second clear run all the way to the grave. Which, when the hunted human sees it very near at hand, he commonly stops of set purpose, and this thing that has chased him catches him up and eats him, even as did the other. Millions are seen to pursue this lust-hunted course, and some even try to combine it with that other sort of money-devil-huntedness. But the advice is given to all in youth that they must make up their minds which of the two sorts of exercise they would choose, and the first is commonly praised and thought worthy; the second blamed. Why, I do not know. Our elders say to us, 'Boy, choose the Money-Devil, give that Lord his run.' Both kinds of sport have seemed to me most miserable, but then I speak only for myself, and I am eccentric in the holidays I choose and the felicity I discover for myself in the conduct of my years.

'For, so far as I am concerned, my pleasure is found rather in having a game with that Great Three-toed Sloth, which is the most amiable of hell's emissaries, and all my life have I played the jolly game of tickling him forward and lolloping in front of him, now lying down until he has caught me up, and then slouching off until he came near again, and even at times making a spurt that I might have the longer sleep at the end, and give honest Sloth a good long waddle for his money.

'Yet after all, my method is the same as every one else's, and will have the same end.

'For when I see the grave a long way off, then do I mean to put on slippers and to mix myself a great bowl of mulled wine with nutmegs, and to fill a pipe, and to sit me down in a great arm-chair before a fire of oak or beech, burning in a great hearth, within sound of the Southern Sea.

'And as I sit there, drinking my hot wine and smoking my long pipe, and watching the fire, and remembering old storms and landfalls far away, I shall hear the plodding and the paddling and the shuffling and the muffling of that great Sloth, my life's pursuer, and he will butt at my door with his snout, but I shall have been too lazy to lock it, and so shall he come in. Then the Great Three-toed Sloth will eat me up, and thus shall *I* find the end of my being and have reached the best thing in the world.'

Myself. 'While you were speaking, Sailor, it seemed to me you had forgotten one great felicity, manly purpose, and final completion of the immortal spirit, which is surely the digging of holes and the filling of them up again.'

The Sailor. 'You are right! I had forgotten that! It is indeed an admirable pastime, and for some, perhaps for many, it is the best thing in the world!'

Myself. 'Yes, indeed, for consider how we drink to thirst again, and eat to hunger again, and love for disappointment, and journey in order to return. And consider with what elaborate care we cut, clip, shave, remove and prune our hair and beard, which none the less will steadfastly re-grow, and how we earn money to spend it, and black boots before walking in the mire, and do penance before sinning, and sleep to wake, and wake to sleep; and very elaborately do pin, button, tie, hook, hang, lace, draw, pull up, be-tighten, and in diverse ways fasten about ourselves our very complicated clothes of a morning, only to un-button, unpin, untie, unhook, let down, be-loosen, and in a thousand operations put them off again when midnight comes. Then there is the soiling of things for their cleansing, and the building of houses to pull them down again, and the making of wars for defeat or for barren victories, and the painting of pictures for the rich blind, and the singing of songs for the wealthy deaf, and the living of all life to the profit of others, and the begetting of children who may perpetuate all that same round. The more I think of it the more I see that the digging of holes and the filling of them up again is the true end of man and his felicity.'

The Poet. 'I think you must be wrong.'

Myself. 'Well then, since you know, what is the best thing in the world?'

The Poet. 'It is a mixture wherein should be compounded and intimately mixed great wads of unexpected money, new land-scapes, and the return of old loves.'

The Sailor. 'Oh, hear him with his return of old loves! All coming in procession, two by two, like the old maids of Midhurst trooping out of church of a Sunday morning! One would think he had slain a hundred with his eye!'

Grizzlebeard. 'All you young men talk folly. The best thing in the world is sleep.'

And having said so much, Grizzlebeard stretched himself upon the bench along one side of the fire, and, pulling his blanket over his head, he would talk to us no more. And we also after a little while, lying huddled in our coats before the blaze, slept hard. And so we passed the hours till morning; now waking in the cold to start a log, then sleeping again. And all night long the wind sounded in the trees.

THE THIRTY-FIRST OF
OCTOBER 1902

THE THIRTY-FIRST OF OCTOBER

1902

I woke next morning to the noise, the pleasant noise, of water boiling in a kettle. May God bless that noise and grant it to be the most sacred noise in the world. For it is the noise that babes hear at birth and that old men hear as they die in their beds, and it is the noise of our households all our long lives long; and throughout the world, wherever men have hearths, that purring and that singing, and that humming and that talking to itself of warm companionable water to our great ally, the fire, is home.

So thought I, half awake, and half asleep upon the hard dry earth of that floor. Yet, as I woke, my mind, not yet in Sussex, thought I was sleeping in an open field, and that there were round me comrades of the regiment, and that the embers that warmed my feet were a bivouac fire. Then I sat up, broad awake, and stiff after such a lodging, to find the Sailor crouching over the renewed flames of two stout logs on which he had established a kettle and water from a spring. He had also with him a packet of tea and some sugar, a loaf, and a little milk.

Grizzlebeard, stiff and stark upon his back along the bench, his head fallen flat, unsupported, his mouth open, breathing but slightly, seemed like a man dead. As for the Poet, he lay bunched up as would a man who had got the last bit of warmth he could; and he was still in a dead sleep, right up against the further corner of the fire.

I shook my coat from me and stood up.

'Sailor,' I said, 'how long have you been awake?'

To which the sailor answered:

'Ever since I was born: worse luck! I never sleep.'

'Where did you get those things,' said I, 'that tea, that milk, that sugar, and that loaf?'

I yawned as I said it, and then I stretched my hands, which sleep had numbed, towards the rising life of the fire. The Sailor was still crouching at the kettle as he answered me slowly and with care:

'Why, you must know that near this house there lives a Troll, who many many years ago when he was young was ensnared by the love of a Fairy, upon that heath called Over-the-world. And he brought her home to be his bride, and lives close by here in a hut that is not of this world. He is my landlord, as it were, and he it was that gave me this tea, this milk, this sugar, and this loaf, but it is no good your asking where; for no one can find that warlock house of theirs but me.'

'That was a long lie to tell,' said I, 'for I certainly should not have bothered myself to find out where the things came from, so only that I can get them free.'

'You are right,' said the Sailor, 'and I also got them free.'

And having said that he upset the packet of tea, and the sugar, and the milk, right into the kettle, so that I cried out to him in alarm:

'What are you at?'

But he told me, as he took the kettle off:

'That is the way the Troll-tea was brewed by the Master-maid upon the heath called Over-the-world. I have been there, so I know.'

And with that he gave a great kick at the Poet, who sat up suddenly from his lump of clothes, looked wild for a moment, then knew where he was, and said 'Oh!'

'It doesn't rhyme,' said the Sailor, 'but you shall have some tea.'

He poured out from the kettle, into the common mug we carried, a measure of the tea, and with his jack-knife he cut off a slice of bread.

Our talk had awakened Grizzlebeard. That older man rose painfully from sleep, as though to see the day again were not to one of his years any very pleasing thing. He sat upon the bench, and for him, as to the one of honour, the tea was next poured out into that silver mug of his, and then was handed to him the next slice of bread. Then I drank and ate, and then the Sailor, and when all this was done we made things orderly in the hut, the Sailor and I. We folded the blankets and stood up the unburnt logs. We poured the kettle out and drank the milk, and stood the loaf upon the ingle-nook, and bidding farewell to that unknown place we left it, to converse with it no more. But the reason we had to put all things in order so, was (the Sailor told me) that if we angered the Troll he might never let us sleep there again.

'You are wonderful company, Sailor!' said I.

'For others, perhaps,' said he, as he locked the door and put the key in his pocket, 'but not for myself; and yet that is the only thing that matters!'

By this time we were all upon the forest path again, turning this way and that as the Sailor might lead us. Sometimes we crossed a great ride without turning down it, and once the broad high road. But we went straight across that, and we passed many signs where it said that any common man found in these woods would be imprisoned, and somewhere it said that any one not rich and yet wandering here might find themselves killed by engines. But the Sailor dodged his way nimbly about, making westward through it all, but so cunningly that even I, who know my County well, grew puzzled. I could not guess in what part of the wood we were until we came to a bottom through which a stream ran, and then I knew that this stream was the rising of the Mole, and that we were in Tilgate. Then I said to my companions: 'Now the woods smell of home!'

But Grizzlebeard said that, considering what the world was

like outside the County, all the County was home. And the Poet said that here were homing bits in the forest, and there were homing bits, and others that were stranger to him, and had not the spirit of our land.

But the Sailor said nothing, only leading us forward by clever paths so that the servants of the rich could not do us any hurt, and then he got us into an open glade, and there we sat and rested for a moment, with our breath drawing in the morning.

For the morning was not as the night had been, full of wind and hurrying clouds, but it was the morning after a gale, in which, on these high hills and among these lifting trees, the air was ambassadorial, bringing a message of life from the sea. But it was a halted air. It no longer followed in the procession of the gale, but was steady and arrived. So that the sky above us was not clouded, and had in it no sign of movement, but was pale with a wintry blue. And there was a frost and a bite all about, although it was so early in the year and winter hardly come. But the leaves had fallen early that year, and the forest was already desolate.

When we had rested ourselves a moment in this glade we followed the Sailor again by a path which presently he left, conducting us with care through untouched underwood, until we came to a hedge, and there across the hedge was the great main road and Pease Pottage close at hand.

'I have led you through this wood,' the Sailor said, 'and now you may take what road you will.'

Myself. 'Now, indeed, I know every yard of the way; and I will take you down towards our own country. But I will take you in my own fashion, for I know the better places, and the quiet lands, and a roof under which we shall be free to sleep at evening. You shall follow me.'

'You know all this?' said Grizzlebeard to me curiously, 'then can you tell me why all these woods are called St. Leonard's Forest?'

Myself. 'Why, certainly; they are called St. Leonard's Forest after St. Leonard.'

The Poet. 'Are you so sure?'

Myself. 'Without a doubt! For it is certain that St. Leonard lived here, and had a little hermitage in the days when poor men might go where they willed. And this hermitage was in that place to which I shall presently take you, from which it is possible to worship at once both our County, and God who made it.'

Saying which I took them along the side road which starts from Pease Pottage (and in those days the old inn was there), but before doing so I asked them severally whether they had any curse on them which forbade them to drink ale of a morning.

This all three of them denied, so we went into the Swan (which in those days I say again was the old inn), and we drank ale, as St. Leonard himself was used to do, round about nine or ten o'clock of an autumn morning. For he was born in these parts, and never went out of the County except once to Germany, when he would convert the heathen there; of whom, returning, he said that if it should please God he would rather be off to hell to convert devils, but that anyhow he was tired of wandering, and thereupon set up his hermitage in the place to which I was now leading my companions.

For when we had gone about a mile by the road I knew, we came to that place where the wood upon the left ends sharply upon that height and suddenly beneath one's feet the whole County lies revealed.

There, a day's march away to the south, stood the rank of the Downs.

No exiles who have seen them thus, coming back after many years, and following the road from London to the sea, hungry for home, were struck more suddenly or more suddenly uplifted by that vision of their hills than we four men so coming upon it that morning, and I was for the moment their leader; for this was a place I had cherished ever since I was a boy.

'Look,' said I to Grizzlebeard, 'how true it is that in this very spot a man might set his seat whence-from to worship all that he saw, and God that must have made it.'

'You are right,' said Grizzlebeard, 'I see before me the Weald in a tumbled garden, Wolstonbury above New Timber and Highden and Rackham beyond' (for these are the names of the

high hills), 'and far away westward I see under Duncton the
Garden of Eden, I think, to which we are bound. And sitting
crowned in the middle place I see Chanctonbury, which, I think,
a dying man remembers so fixed against the south, if he is a man
from Ashurst, or from Thakeham, or from the pine-woods by the
rock, whenever by some evil-fortune a Sussex man dies far away
from home.'

'Tell me,' said the Sailor, 'can you fix for us here the place
where St. Leonard built his hermitage?'

'Certainly,' said I, and they gathered round.

'Here,' said I, 'was the *cella*' (drawing a circle with my stick
upon the ground), 'and here' (moving off a yard or two) 'was his
narthex or *carfax*, as some call it, and here to the right' (and here I
moved backwards and drew my stick across some sand) 'was the
bibulatium; but all the ruins of this monument have disappeared
through quarrying and the effects of time, saving always such
traces as can be distinguished by experts, and I am one.'

Then, wishing to leave them no time for wrangling, I took
them down away through Shelley Plain, and when I had gone a
mile or so I said:

'Is not the river to which we are bound the river of Arun?'

The Poet. 'Why, yes. If it were not so I would never have
joined you.'

The Sailor. 'Certainly we are bound for Arun, which, when a
man bathes in it, makes him forget everything that has come upon
him since his eighteenth year—or possibly his twenty-seventh.'

'Yes,' said Grizzlebeard, more gravely, 'we are bound for the
river of Arun, which is as old as it is young, and therein we hope
to find our youth, and to discover once again the things we knew.'

'Why, then,' said I, 'let me mock you and cover you with disil-
lusion, and profane your shrines, and disappoint your pilgrimage! For that trickle of water below you to the left in the dale,
and that long lake you see with a lonely wood about either shore,
is the place where Arun rises.'

Grizzlebeard. 'That is nothing to me as we go along our way.
It is not little baby Arun that I come to see, but Arun in his
majesty, married to salt water, and a king.'

The Sailor. 'For my part I am glad to have assisted at the nativity of Arun. Prosper, beloved river! It is your business (not mine) if you choose to go through so many doubtful miles of youth, and to grope uncertainly towards fruition and the sea.'

The Poet. 'There is always some holiness in the rising of rivers, and a great attachment to their springs.'

By this time we had come to the lake foot, where a barrier holds in the water, and the road crosses upon a great dam. And we watched as we passed it the plunge of the cascade; and then passing over that young river we went up over the waste land to the height called Lower Beeding, which means the lower place of prayer, and is set upon the very summit of a hill. Just as Upper Beeding is at the very lowest point in the whole County of Sussex, right down, down, down upon the distant marshes of Adur, flush, as you may say, with the sea.

For when Adam set out (with the help of Eve) to name all the places of the earth (and that is why he had to live so long), he desired to distinguish Sussex, late his happy seat, by some special mark which would pick it out from all the other places of the earth, its inferiors and vassals. So that when Paradise might be regained and the hopeless generation of men permitted to pass the Flaming Sword at Shiremark Mill, and to see once more the four rivers, Arun and Adur, and Cuckmere and Ouse, they might know their native place again and mark it for Paradise. And the best manner (thought Adam) so to establish by names this good peculiar place, this Eden which is Sussex still, was to make her names of a sort that should give fools to think. So he laid it down that whatever was high in Sussex should be called low, and whatever was low should be called high, and that a hill should be called a plain, and a bank should be called a ditch, and the North wood should be south of the Downs, and the Nore Hill south of the wood, and Southwater north of them all, and that no one in the County should pronounce 'th,' 'ph,' or 'sh,' but always 'h' separately, under pain of damnation. And that names should have their last letters weighed upon, contrariwise to the custom of all England.

So much for our names, which any man may prove for himself
by considering Bos-ham, and Felp-ham, and Hors-ham, and
Arding-ly, and the square place called 'Roundabout.' Or the
Broadbridge, which is so narrow that two carts cannot pass on it.
God knows we are a single land!

We had passed then, we four (and hungry, and stepping
strongly, for it was downhill), we had passed under the cold pure
air of that good day from Lower Beeding down the hill past
Leonard's Lee, and I was telling my companions how we might
hope to eat and drink at the Crabtree or at Little Cowfold, when
the Sailor suddenly began to sing in a manner so loud and joyful
that in some more progressive place than the County he would
most certainly have been thrown into prison. But the occasion of
his song was a good one, for debouching through the wooded part
of the road we had just come upon that opening whence once
more, though from a lower height, the open Weald and the mag-
nificence of the Downs is spread out to glorify men's eyes. He
sang that song, which is still native to this land, through all the
length of it, and we who had heard it each in our own place first
helped him with the chorus, and then swelled it altogether in
diverse tones. He beginning:

I

On Sussex hills where I was bred,
When lanes in autumn rains are red,
When Arun tumbles in his bed,
   And busy great gusts go by;
When branch is bare in Burton Glen
And Bury Hill is a whitening, then,
I drink strong ale with gentlemen;
     Which nobody can deny, deny,
       Deny, deny, deny, deny,
         Which nobody can deny!

II

In half-November off I go,
To push my face against the snow,
And watch the winds wherever they blow,
   Because my heart is high:
Till I settle me down in Steyning to sing
Of the women I met in my wandering,
And of all that I mean to do in the spring.
     Which nobody can deny, deny,
       Deny, deny, deny, deny,
         Which nobody can deny!

III

Then times be rude and weather be rough,
And ways be foul and fortune tough,
We are of the stout South Country stuff,
   That never can have good ale enough,
   And do this chorus cry!
From Crowboro' Top to Ditchling Down,
From Hurstpierpoint to Arundel town,
The girls are plump and the ale is brown:
     Which nobody can deny, deny,
       Deny, deny, deny, deny!
         If he does he tells a lie!

When we had all done singing and were near the Crabtree, the Sailor said:

'Now, was not that a good song?'

'Yes,' said I, 'and well suited to this morning and to this air, and to that broad sight of the lower land which now spreads out before us.'

For even as I spoke we had come to that little shelf on which the Crabtree stands, and from which one may see the Downs all stretched before one, and Bramber Gap, and in the notch of it the high roof of Lancing; and then onwards, much further away, Arundel Gap and the hills and woods of home. It was certainly in the land beneath us, and along the Weald, which we over-looked, that once, many years ago, a young man must have written this song.

Grizzlebeard. 'In what places, Myself, do you find that you can sing?'

Myself. 'In any place whatsoever.'

The Sailor. 'As, for instance, at the table of some rich money-lending man who has a few men friends to dinner that night, with whom he would discuss Affairs of State, and who has only asked you because you were once a hanger-on of his great-nephew's. This would seem to me an excellent occasion on which to sing "Golier!"'

The Poet. 'Yes, or again, when you are coming (yourself small and unknown) to the reception of some wealthy hostess from whom you expect advancement. It was in such a place and at such a time that Charlie Ribston, now in jail, did first so richly produce his song, "The Wowly Wows," which has that jolly chorus to it.'

Grizzlebeard. 'The reason I asked you where you could sing was, that I thought it now impossible in any place, I mean in this realm, and in our dreadful time. For is there not a law, and is it not in force, whereby any man singing in the open, if he be overheard by the police, shall be certified by two doctors, imprisoned, branded, his thumbs marks taken, his hair shaved off, one of his eyes put out, all his money matters carefully gone into backwards and forwards, and, in proportion to the logarithm of his income, a large tax laid on? And after all this the duty laid upon him under heavy pains of reporting himself every month to a local committee, with the parson's wife up top, and to a politician's jobber, and to all such other authorities as may see fit, pursuant to the majesty of our Lord the King, his crown and dignity? I seem to have heard something of the kind.'

'Yes, you are right enough,' said I; 'but when a man comes to lonely places, which are like islands and separate from this sea of tyranny, as, for instance, this road by Leonard's Lee, why a man can still sing.'

The Sailor. 'Yes, and in an inn.'

'In a few inns,' said I, 'under some conditions and at certain times.'

Grizzlebeard. 'Very well, we will choose upon this march of ours such inns and such times. And is this one?' he added, pointing to the Crabtree.

'Not outside,' I answered cautiously, 'nor at this hour.'

'However,' said the Poet, 'we will eat.'

So we sat outside there upon the benches of the Crabtree Inn, eating bread and cheese.

Now when we had eaten our bread and cheese in that cold, still air, and overlooking so great a scene below us, and when we had drunk yet more of the ale, and also of a port called Jubilee (for the year of Jubilee was, at the time this walk was taken, not more than five years past), the Sailor said in a sort of challenging tone:

'You were saying, I think, that a man could only sing to-day in certain lonely places, such as all down that trim hedgerow, which is the roadside of Leonard's Lee, and when Grizzlebeard here asked whether a man might sing outside the Crabtree, you said no. But I will make the experiment; and by way of compromise, so that no one may be shocked, my song shall be of a religious sort, dealing with the great truths. And perhaps that will soften the heart of the torturers, if indeed they have orders, as you say, to persecute men for so simple a thing as a song.'

Grizzlebeard. 'If your song is one upon the divinities, it will not go with ale and with wine, nor with the character of an inn.'

The Sailor. 'Do not be so sure. Wait until you have heard it. For this song that I am proposing to sing is of a good loud roaring sort, but none the less it deals with the ultimate things, and you

must know that it is far more than one thousand years old.   Now
it cannot be properly sung unless the semi-chorus (which I will
indicate by raising my hands) is sung loudly by all of you together, nor unless the chorus is bellowed by the lot of you for
dear life's sake, until the windows rattle and the populace rise.
Such is the nature of the song.'

   Having said so much then, the Sailor, leaning back, began in a
very full and decisive manner to sing this

*Song of the Pelagian Heresy for the Strengthening of Men's Backs and the
very Robust Out-thrusting of Doubtful Doctrine and the Uncertain
Intellectual.*

Pelagius lived in Kardanoel,
  And taught a doctrine there,
How whether you went to Heaven or Hell,
  It was your own affair.
How, whether you found eternal joy
  Or sank forever to burn,
It had nothing to do with the Church, my boy,
  But was your own concern.

Grizzlebeard. 'This song is blasphemous.'
The Sailor. 'Not at all—the exact contrary, it is orthodox. But now I beg of you do not interrupt, for this is the semi-chorus.'

[*Semi-chorus.*]

Oh, he didn't believe
In Adam and Eve,
  He put no faith therein!
His doubts began
With the fall of man,
  And he laughed at original sin!

In this semi-chorus we all joined, catching it up as he went along, and then the Sailor, begging us to put all our manhood into it, launched upon the chorus itself, which was both strong and simple.

[*Chorus.*]

With my row-ti-tow, ti-oodly-ow,
  He laughed at original sin!

When we had got as far as this, which was the end of the first verse, and defines the matter in hand, the very extravagant noise of it all brought out from their dens not a few of the neighbourhood, who listened and waited to see what would come. But the Sailor, not at all abashed, continued, approaching the second verse.

> Whereat the Bishop of old Auxerre
>   (Germanus was his name),
> He tore great handfuls out of his hair,
>   And he called Pelagius Shame:
> And then with his stout Episcopal staff
>   So thoroughly thwacked and banged
> The heretics all, both short and tall,
>   They rather had been hanged.

[*Semi-chorus.*]

> Oh, he thwacked them hard, and he banged them long,
>   Upon each and all occasions,
> Till they bellowed in chorus, loud and strong,
>   Their orthodox persuasions!

[*Chorus.*]

> With my row-ti-tow, ti-oodly-ow,
>   Their orthodox persua-a-a-sions!

At the end of this second verse the crowd had grown greater, and not a few of them had dropped their lower jaws and stood with their mouths wide open, never having heard a song of this kind before. But the Sailor, looking kindly upon them, and nodding at them, as much as to say, 'You will understand it all in a minute,' took on the third verse, with still greater gusto, and sang:

> Now the Faith is old and the Devil is bold,
>   Exceedingly bold indeed;
> And the masses of doubt that are floating about
>   Would smother a mortal creed.
> But we that sit in a sturdy youth,
>   And still can drink strong ale,
> Oh—let us put it away to infallible truth,
>   Which always shall prevail!

[*Semi-chorus.*]

> And thank the Lord
> For the temporal sword,
>   And howling heretics too;
> And whatever good things
> Our Christendom brings,
>   But especially barley brew!

[*Chorus.*]
>   With my row-ti-tow, ti-oodly-ow,
>   Especially barley brew!

When we had finished this last chorus in a louder mode than all the rest, you may say that half the inhabitants of that hill were standing round. But the Sailor, rising smartly and putting money down upon the table to pay for our fare and somewhat over, bade us all rise with him, which we did, and then he spoke thus to the assembly:

'Good people! I trust you clearly heard every word of what we have just delivered to you, for it is Government business, and we were sent to give it to you just as we had ourselves received it of the Cabinet, whose envoys we are. And let me add for your comfort that this same Government of our Lord the King (his crown and dignity), ever solicitous for the welfare of poorer folk, has given us monies wherewith to refresh all the people of Sussex all our way along. On which account I have left here upon the table, in the name of the aforesaid Right Honourables, a sum of five shillings, against which you may order ale to the breaking point, and so good-day to you. But you are strictly charged that you do not follow us or molest us in any fashion, to the offence of those good Ministers who lie awake at night, considering the good of the people, and the service of our Lord the King (his crown and dignity). Oyez! Le Roi le veult!'

And having said this he beckoned us to follow him, and as we strode down the road we heard them all cheering loudly, for they thought that time had come which is spoken of by the Prophet Habakkuk, 'When the poor shall be filled and the rich shall be merry.' A thing that never yet was since the beginning of the world.

*

As we swung down the road which leads at last to Little Cowfold, Grizzlebeard, thinking about that song, said:

'I cannot believe, Sailor, that your song is either old or true; for there is no such place as Kardanoel, and Pelagius never lived

there, and his doctrine was very different from what you say, and
the blessed Germanus would not have hurt a fly. As witness that
battle of his somewhere in Flint, where he discomforted the
Scotch, of all people, by talking Hebrew too loud, although he
only knew one word of the tongue. Then, also, what you say of
ale is not ecclesiastical, nor is it right doctrine to thank the Lord
for heresy.'

The Sailor. 'Anything you will! But every church must have
its customs within reason, and this song, or rather hymn, is of
Breviary, and very properly used in the diocese of Theleme upon
certain feast days. Yes, notably that of Saints Comus and
Hilarius, who, having nothing else to do, would have been
cruelly martyred for the faith had they not contrariwise, as befits
Christian men, be-martyred and banged to death their very per-
secutors in turn. It is a prose of the church militant, and is as-
cribed to Dun-Scotus, but is more probably of traditional origin.
Compare the 'Hymn to the Ass,' which all good Christian men
should know.'

Grizzlebeard. 'Nevertheless I doubt if it be for the strengthening of souls, but rather a bit of ribaldry, more worthy of the
Martyrs' Mount which you may know, than of holy Sussex.'

When we had come to Little Cowfold, which we did very
shortly, it was already past three in the afternoon, and therefore
in such early weather (more wintry than autumn) the air had a
touch of evening, and looking at the church there and admiring it,
we debated whether we would stop in that place a little while and
pick a quarrel with any one, or lacking that, sing another song, or
lacking that, drink silently. For Virgil says, 'Propria quae
Cowfold Carmen Cervisia Ludus.'

But as it was so late we thought we would not do any of these
things, but take the way along to Henfield and get us near to the
Downs, though how far we should go that night we none of us
could tell. Only we were settled on this, that by the next day,
which would be All-Hallows, we must come upon the river Arun
and the western part of the County, and all the things we knew.

So we went on southward towards Henfield, and as we went,
Grizzlebeard, who was striding strongly, reminded us that it was

All Halloween. On this night of all nights in the year there is most stir and business among the things that are not seen by men, and there is a rumour in all the woods; and very late, when men are sleeping, all those who may not come to earth at any other time, come and hold their revels. The Little People who are good for the most part, dance this night in the meadows and undergrowth, and move in and out of the reeds along the river bank, and twine round and round in rings, holding hands upon the flat pastures, the water meadows, and the heaths that are nearer the sea. It is this dancing of theirs that leaves upon the grass its track in a brighter green, and marks the fields with those wheels and circles which convince unbelieving men.

The Poet said that he had seen the Little People, but we knew that what he said was false.

Grizzlebeard said that though he had not seen them he believed, in reward for which the Little People had blest him all his life. And that was why (he told us) he was so rich, for though his father had left him plenty, the Little People had increased it, because he had neither doubted them nor ever wished them ill.

The Sailor. 'Then you were lucky! For it is well known that those who come upon the Little People dancing round and round are caught by them in the middle of the ring. And the Little People laugh at them with a noise like very small silver bells. And then, as though to make amends for their laughter, they lead the mortal away to a place where one can go underground. And when they get there, in a fine hall where the Queen sits with Oberon, it is ordered that the man shall be given gold. They bring him a sack, and he stuffs it full of the gold pieces, full to the neck, and he shoulders it and makes to thank them, when, quite suddenly, he finds he is no longer in that hall, but on the open heath at early morning with no one about, and in an air quite miserably cold. Then that man, shivering and wondering whether ever he saw the Little People or no, says to himself, 'At least I have my gold.' But when he goes to take the sack up again he finds it very light, and pouring out from it upon the ground he gets, instead of the gold they gave him, nothing but dead leaves: the round dead leaves and brown of the beech, and of the hornbeam, for it is of this sort that they mint the fairy gold. They say that as he leaves it there, disappointed and angry at his adventure, he seems to hear again, though it is daylight, far down beneath the ground, the slight tinkle of many tiny silver bells, and knows that it is the Little People laughing.'

Grizzlebeard. 'So it may be for those who have the great misfortune to see the Little People, but, as I told you, I have never seen them, and with me it has been the other way about. Year after year have I picked up the dead leaves, until all the leaves of my life were dead, and year after year I have found between my hands gold and more gold.'

The Poet. 'I tell you again I have seen them, and when I was a younger man I saw them often, and I would be with them for hours in that good place of theirs where nothing matters very much and no one goes away.'

The Sailor. 'And what did they give you beyond that loon look which is the mark of all your tribe?'

The Poet. 'Why, they gave me the power to conceive good verse, and this I still retain.'

The Sailor. 'Now indeed, Poet, I believe, which I did not at first, that you have seen the Little People. For what you have just said proves it to me. You also have handled fairy gold—and there are many like you. For the Little People gave you verse that seemed well minted, sterling, and sound, and you put it into your sack and you bore it away. But when you came out into man's-world and tasted the upper air, then, as all your hearers and your readers know, this verse turned out to be the light and worthless matter of dead leaves. Oh, do not shake your head! We know that verse of youth which the fairies give us in mockery; only we, when we grow up, are too wise to cherish the bag-full. We leave it for the wind to scatter, for it is all dead leaves. Only you poets hang on to your bag and clutch it and carry it with you, making fools of yourselves all your lives long, while we sturdy fellows in a manly fashion turn to the proper things of men in man's-world, and take to lawyering and building, and the lending of money and horse-doping, and every other work that befits a man.'

Grizzlebeard. 'And you, Myself, have you ever seen the Fairies?'

Myself. 'I do not think so. I do not think I have ever seen them: alas for me! But I think I have heard them once or twice, murmuring and chattering, and pattering and clattering, and flattering and mocking at me, and alluring me onwards towards the perilous edges and the water-ledges where the torrent tumbles and cascades in the high hills.'

The Sailor. 'What did they say to you?'

Myself. 'They told me I should never get home, and I never have.'

As we so talked the darkness began to gather, for we had waited once or twice by the way, and especially at that little lift in the road where one passes through a glen of oaks and sees before one great flat water meadows, and beyond them the high Downs quite near.

The sky was already of an apple green to the westward, and in the eastern blue there were stars. There also shone what had not yet appeared upon that windless day, a few small wintry clouds, neat and defined in heaven. Above them the moon, past her first quarter but not yet full, was no longer pale, but began to make a cold glory; and all that valley of Adur was a great and solemn sight to see as we went forward upon our adventure that led nowhere and away. To us four men, no one of whom could know the other, and who had met by I could not tell what chance, and would part very soon for ever, these things were given. All four of us together received the sacrament of that wide and silent beauty, and we ourselves went in silence to receive it.

*

And so when it was full dark we came to Henfield, and determined that it was time for bread, and for bacon, and for ale—a night meal inspired by the road and by the tang of the cold. For you must know that once again, though it was yet so early in the year, a very slight frost had nipped the ground.

We made therefore for an inn in that place, and asked the mistress of it to fry us bacon, and with it to give us bread and as much ale as four men could drink by her judgment and our own; and while we sat there, waiting for this meal, the Sailor said to me:

'Come, now, Myself, since you say that you know the County so well, can you tell us how Hog is made so suitable to Man?'

Grizzlebeard. 'Why, no man can tell that, for we only know that these things are so. But some men say that in the beginning the horse was made for man to ride, and the cow for man to milk, and the hog for man to eat; with wheat also, which was given him to sow in a field, just as those stars and that waxing moon were given him to lift his eyes towards heaven, and the sun to give him light and warmth by day. But others say that all things are a jumble, and that the stars care nothing for us, and that the moon, if only the truth were known, is a very long way off, and a useless beast (God forgive me! It is not I that speak thus, but they!), and that we just happened upon horses (which I can well believe when I see some men ride), and that even that most-perfectly-fitting creature and manifestly-adapted-to-man, that hale four-footed one, the Hog, was but an accident, and is not an end in himself for us, but may, in the change of human affairs, be replaced by some other more suitable thing. All things are made for an end, but who shall say what end?'

Myself. 'Those who talk thus, Grizzlebeard, have not carefully considered the works of man, nor his curious ways, which betray in him the reflection of his Creator, and mark him for an artist. The curing of Hog Flesh till it became bacon is a sure evidence of the creed. There are those, I know, who still pretend that the pin and the needle, the hammer and the saw, and even the violin, grew up and were fashioned bit by bit, man stumbling towards them from experiment to experiment. At these atheists I howl, believing verily and without doubt that in the beginning, when grandfather and grandmother were turned out of Eden, and were compelled by some Order in Council or other to leave this County (but we are now returned), they were very kindly presented by the authorities with the following:

One tool-box.

A cock and six hens.

Some paint and brushes and a tube of sepia.

Six pencils, running from BB. to 4H.

Tobacco in a tin.

A Greek Grammar and Lexicon.

Half-hours with the best writers of English verse and
    prose, excluding thing-um-bob.

A little printing-press.

A Bible.

The Elements of Jurisprudence.

A compact travelling medicine chest.

A collection of seeds, with

A pamphlet that should accompany these, and

Two Pigs.

'These last also were saved in the Ark, as witness Holy Writ, and one of them later accompanied St. Anthony, and is his ritual beast on every monument.'

'But all this,' said the Sailor, as he began eating his bacon, 'tells us nothing of the curing of pigs, which art, you say, is a proof of man's original instruction, and of the intentions of Providence.'

Myself. 'And I said it very truly, for how of himself could man have discovered such a thing? There is revelation about it, and the seeming contradiction which inhabits all mysterious gifts.'

Grizzlebeard. 'You mean that there is no curing a pig until the pig is dead? For though that is the very moment when our materialists would say that he was past all healing, yet (oh, marvel!) that is the very time most suitable for curing him.'

The Poet. 'Well, but beyond the theology of the matter, will you not tell us how a pig is cured, for I long to learn one useful thing in my life.'

Myself. 'You will not learn it in the mere telling; for what says the Philosopher? "If you would be a Carpenter you must do Carpenter's work." However, for the enduring affection I bear you, and also for my delight in the art, I will expound this thing.

'First, then, you cut your pig in two, and lay each half evenly and fairly upon a smooth well-washed board of deal, oak, ash,

elm, walnut, teak, mahogany, ebony, rosewood, or any other
kind of wood; and then, taking one such half you put by on one
side a heap of saltpetre, and gathering a handful of this saltpetre
you very diligently rub it into the flesh, and, rubbing, have a care
to rub it rubbedly, as rub should, and show yourself a master
rubber at rubbing. And all this you must do on the inside and
not on the out, for that is all covered over with hair.

'When, therefore, you have so rubbed in a rubbard manner
until your rubment is aglow with the rubbing, why then desist;
hang up your half pig on a hook from a beam, and wash your
hands and have done for that day.

'But next day you must begin again in the same manner (having
first consecrated your work by a prayer), and so on for thirty
days; but each day a little less than the last, until, before the
curing is ended, you are taking but a tithe of the saltpetre you
took at the beginning.

'When all this is over your half pig is as stiff as a prude, and as
salt as sorrow, and as incorruptible as a lawyer, and as tough as
Tacitus. Then may you lift it up all of one piece, like a log, and
put it to smoke over a wood fire, as the giants did in old time, or
you may pack it between clean layers of straw, as the Germans do
to this day, or you may do whatever you will, and be damned to
it; for no matter what you do, you will still have a pig of pigs, and
a pork perfect, that has achieved its destiny and found the fruit of
its birth: a scandal to Mahound, and food for Christian men.'

The Sailor. 'All that you say is true enough, but what of the
bristles of the pig? What of his hair? Are not bristles better in
brushes than in bacon?'

Myself. 'You speak truth soundly, though perhaps a little
sharply, when you ask, 'How about hair?' For the pig, like all
brutes, differs from man in this, that his hide is covered with
hair. On which theme also the poet Wordsworth, or some such
fellow, composed a poem, which, as you have not previously
heard it, let me now tell you (in the fashion of Burnand) I shall at
once proceed to relate; and I shall sing it in that sort of voice
called by Italians "The Tenore Stridente," but by us a Hearty
Stave.'

The dog is a faithful, intelligent friend,
  But his hide is covered with hair;
The cat will inhabit the house to the end,
  But *her* hide is covered with hair.

  The hide of the mammoth was covered with wool,
  The hide of the porpoise is sleek and cool,
  But you'll find, if you look at that gambolling fool,
    That his hide is covered with hair.

Oh, I thank my God for this at the least,
I was born in the West and not in the East,
And He made me a human instead of a beast,
  Whose hide is covered with hair!

  Grizzlebeard (*with interest*).   'This song is new to me, although I
know most songs.   Is it your own?'

Myself. 'Why, no, it's a translation, but a free one I admit, from Anacreon or Theocritus, I forgot which . . . What am I saying? Is it not Wordsworth's, as we said just now? There is so much of his that is but little known! Would you have further verses? There are many . . .'

The Sailor. 'No.'

Myself. 'Why, then, I will immediately continue.

> The cow in the pasture that chews the cud,
> Her hide is covered with hair.'

The Sailor. 'Halt!'

> And even a horse of the Barbary blood,
> *His* hide is covered with hair.

> The camel excels in a number of ways,
> And travellers give him unlimited praise—
> He can go without drinking for several days—
> But his hide is covered with hair.

Grizzlebeard. 'How many verses are there of this?'

Myself. 'There are a great number. For all the beasts of the field, and creeping things, and furred creatures of the sea come into this song, and towards the end of it the Hairy Ainu himself. There are hundreds upon hundreds of verses.

> The bear of the forest that lives in a pit,
> His hide is covered with hair;
> The laughing hyena in spite of his wit,
> *His* Hide is covered with hair!

> The Barbary ape and the chimpanzee,
> And the lion of Africa, verily he,
> With his head like a wig, and the tuft on his knee,
> His hide . . .'

Grizzlebeard (*rising*). 'Enough! Enough! These songs, which rival the sea-serpent in length, are no part of the true poetic spirit, and I cannot believe that the conscientious Wordsworth, surnamed ἱπποκέφαλος, or Horse Face, wrote this, nor even that it is any true translation of Anacreon or the shining Theocritus. There is some error! This manner of imagining a theme, to which innumerable chapters may be added in a similar vein, is no part of poetry! It is rather a camp-habit, worthy only of a rude soldiery, to help them along the road and under the heavy pack. For I can understand that in long marches men would have to chant such endless things with a pad and a beat of the foot to them, but not we. I say enough, and enough!'

I answered him, getting up also as he had, and making ready for the road. 'Why, Grizzlebeard, this is not very kind of you, for though you had allowed me but fifteen verses more I could have got through the Greater Carnivoræ, and perhaps, before the closure, we could have brought in the Wart Hog, who loves not war, but is a Pacifist.'

The Poet (*rising also*). 'It may be so, good Myself, but remember that you bear them all in store. Nothing is really lost. You will rediscover these verses in eternity, and no doubt your time in hell will be long enough to exhaust, in series, all the animals that ever were.'

The Sailor (*rising last*). 'Grizzlebeard has saved us all!'

With this condemnation of a noble song they moved out of doors on to the road, a little aimlessly, gazing out towards the high Downs, under the now bright-burnished moon, and doubtful whither they should proceed. Grizzlebeard proposed in a gentle fashion that we should go on to an inn at Bramber and sleep there, but the Sailor suddenly said 'No!'

He said it with such violence and determination that we were all surprised, and looked at him with fear. Then he went on:

'No, we will not go to the inn at Bramber, nor breathe upon embers which are now so nearly extinguished; we will not go and walk in the woods whence all the laurels have been cut away, nor will we return to emotions which in their day were perhaps but vaguely divine, but which the lapse of time has rendered sacred. It is the most perilous of human endeavours, is this attempt to return to the past; should it fail, it breeds the most woeful of human woes. I know as well as you the gardens of Bramber, and I, too, have sat there eating and drinking upon summer evenings between the last light and the dark. I, too, have watched a large star that began to show above Buttolph Combe; and I, also, have seen the flitter-mice darting above me in an air like bronze. Believe me, I have heard the nightingale in Bramber, but I will not return.'

The Poet. 'But——!'

The Sailor. 'Be silent! . . .   I will not return . . .   It was the best of inns! . . .   You talk of the inn at Saint Girons, where the wine was good in the days of Arthur Young, and is still good to-day—not the same wine, but the grandson of the same wine—and you speak favourably of that inn under the pass coming in from Val Carlos. You talk justly of the famous inn at Urgel, known as the Universal Inn, from which a man can watch under a full moon the vast height of the Sierra del Cadi; and you perpetually repeat the praises of the inn at the Sign of the Chain of Gold, under a large ruined castle, by a broad and very peaceful river in Normandy. You do well to praise them, but all these inns together could not even stand at the knees of what was once the inn at Bramber.'

Myself. 'I have never mentioned one of these inns!'

The Sailor. 'There is not upon earth so good a thing as an inn; but even among good things there must be hierarchy. The angels, they say, go by steps, and I am very ready to believe it. It is true also of inns. It is not for a wandering man to put them in their order; but in my youth the best inn of the inns of the world was an inn forgotten in the trees of Bramber. It is on this account that I will not return. The famous Tuscan inns have tempted many men to praise them, some (as I think) extravagantly. And of the lesser inns of seaports sailors (though they never praise in prose or verse) know and speak of the Star of Yarmouth—I mean of Great Yarmouth—and the County Inn of the other Yarmouth—I mean of Little Yarmouth—and especially in loud voices do they commend the Dolphin at Southampton, which is a very noble inn with bow windows, and second to no house in the world for the opportunity of composing admirable verse and fluent prose. Then also, lying inland one day's march from the sea, how many inns have not sailors known! Is there

not the Bridge Inn of Amberley and the White Hart of Storrington, the Spread Eagle of Midhurst, that oldest and most
revered of all the prime inns of this world, and the White Hart of
Steyning and the White Horse of Storrington and the Swan of
Petworth, all of which it may be our business to see? They were
mortal inns, human inns, full of a common and a reasonable
good; but round the inn at Bramber, my companions, there
hangs a very different air. Memory bathes it and the drift of
time, and the perpetual obsession of youth. So let us leave it
there. I will put up the picture of an early love; I will hear with
mixed sorrow and delight the songs that filled my childhood; but
I will not deliberately view that which by a process of sanctifica-
tion through time has come to be hardly of this world. I will not
go sleep in the inn at Bramber—the gods forbid me.

'Nay, apart from all of this which you three perhaps (and
especially the Poet) are not of a stuff to comprehend, apart from
these rare and mysterious considerations, I say, there is an
evident and an easy reason for not stirring the leaves of memory.
Who knows that we should find it the same? Who knows that
the same voices would be heard in that garden, or that the green
paint on the tables would still be dusty, blistered, and old? That
the chairs would still be rickety, and that cucumber would still be
the principal ornament of the feast? Have you not learnt in your
lives, you two that are one young, one middle-aged, and you, the
third, who are quite old, have you not learnt how everything is a
function of motion; how all things only exist because they
change? And what purpose would it serve to shock once more
that craving of the soul for certitude and for repose? With what
poignant and terrible grief should we not wrestle if the contrast of
that which was once the inn at Bramber should rise a terrible
ghost and challenge that which is the inn at Bramber now! Of
what it was and what it has become might there not rise a dual
picture before our minds—a picture that should torture us with
the doom of time? I will not play with passions that are too
strong for men; I will not go sleep to-night at the inn of Bramber.

'Is not the world full of other inns wherein a man can sleep
deeply and wake as it were in a new world? Has not heaven set

for us, like stars in the sky, these points of isolation and repose all
up and down the fields of Christendom? Is there not an inn at
the Land's End where you can lie awake in a rest that is better
than slumber, listening to the noise of the sea upon the Longships
and to the Atlantic wind? And is there not another inn at John o'
Groats to which you may bicycle if you choose (but so shall not
I)? Is there not the nameless inn famous for its burgundy in
Llanidloes? Is there no Unicorn in Machynlleth? Are there not
in Dolgelly forty thousand curious inns and strong? And what
of the Feathers at Ludlow, where men drink so often and so
deeply after the extinguishing of fires, and of its sister inn at
Ledbury? And what of the New Inn at Gloucester, which is
older than the New College at Oxford or the New Bridge at
Paris? And by the way, if Oxford itself have no true inns, are
there not inns hanging like planets in a circle round the town?
The inns of Eynsham, of Shillingford, of Dorchester, of Abing-
don, the remarkable inn at Nuneham, and the detestable inn at
Wheatley which fell from grace some sixty years ago, and now
clearly stands for a mark of reprobation to show what inns may
become, when, though possessed of free will and destined to
eternal joy, they fail to fulfil their hostelarian destiny . . . Yes,
indeed, there are inns enough in the world among which to
choose without being forced by evil fate or still more evil
curiosity to pull out in the organ of the soul the deep but—oh! the
fast and inviolable—the forbidden stops of resurrection and of
accomplished loving. For no man may re-live his youth, nor is
love fruitful altogether to man.'

Grizzlebeard (*musing*). 'If it were not so far I should
proceed this very night to the Station Hotel at York, which
of all the houses I know is the largest and the most
secure.'

The Poet. 'And I to the Fish, Dog, and Duck where the Ouse
comes in to the Cam, or to the Grapes on the hills above Cor-
bridge before you venture upon the loneliness of Northumber-
land; both excellent inns.'

Myself. 'But I, to the sign of the Lion, up on Arun, which no
man knows but me. There should I approach once more the

ancient riddle, and hear, perhaps, at last, the voices of the dead, and know the dooms of the soul.'

The Sailor. 'You would all three do well. For inns are as men and women are, with character and fate infinitely diversified, and to one an old man goes for silence and repose, to another a younger man for adventure or for isolation, to a third a poet for no reason save to lay up a further store of peevish impotence, which is the food upon which these half-men commonly feed. So also there are inns coquettish, inns brutal, inns obvious, inns kindly, and inns strong—each is for a mood. But as in every life there is one emotion which may not be touched and to which the common day is not sufficient, so with inns. For me one is thus sacred, which is that inn at Bramber. Thither therefore, as I think I have said before, I will not go.'

Myself. 'Now that all the affection of your talk is spent, I may tell you that you might have saved your breath, for close at hand I know of a little house, empty but well furnished and full of stores for winter. Sailor—I say this to you—the Trolls are not my friends. Yet of such little houses all up and down the County I alone possess the keys. We will go, then, to this little house of mine, for it is not a mile across the water-meadows.'

This we did, and as we passed the wooden bridge we saw below us my little river, the river Adur, slipping at low tide towards the sea.

*

So we went on over the water-meadows. It was very cold, and the moon rode over Chanctonbury in a clear heaven. We did not speak. We plodded on all four, in single file, myself leading, along the narrow path by the bare hedge-side. The frost had touched the grass, and the twigs of quickset were sharp in the moonlight like things engraved upon metal. We came out upon the Ashurst road. The mill was all sound in those days, and the arms of it stood against the sky. We walked abreast, but still in silence: the Poet slouched and Grizzlebeard let his stick trail along the ground, and even the Sailor had a melancholy air, though his strong legs carried him well. As for me I still pressed

onwards a little ahead of the line, for I knew my goal near at
hand, while for my three companions it was but an aimless trudge
through the darkness after a long day's journey. So did we near
that little house which God knows I love as well as any six or
seven little houses in the world.

We came to the foot of a short hill: tall elms stood out against
the sky a short way back from the road and beyond a little green.
Beneath them shone the thatch of a vast barn, and next it a sight
which I knew very well . . . the roof and chimney. I turned from
the road to cross the green, and I took from my pocket a great
key, and when my companions saw this their merriment returned
to them, for they knew that I had found the shelter.

Grizzlebeard said: 'Look how all doors in the County open to
you!'

'Not all,' I answered, 'but certainly four or five.'

I turned the key in the lock, and there, within, when I had
struck a match, appeared the familiar room. The beam of the
ceiling was a friend to me and the great down-fire-place inhabited
the room. There, in that recess, lay on the dogs and the good
pile of ashes, a faggot and four or five huge logs of cord wood, of
oak from the clay of the Weald: I lit beneath all these a sheaf of
verse I had carried about for months, but which had disappointed me, and the flames leapt up, in shape like leaves of holly.
It was a good sight to see.

With the fire humanity returned; we talked, we spread our
hands; one pulled the curtains over the long low window of the
room, another brought the benches near the blaze, benches with
high backs and dark with age; another put the boards on the
trestles before it; another lit two candles and stood them in their
own grease upon the boards. We were in a new mood, being
come out of the night and seeing the merriment of the fire.

Next we would send to the Fountain for drink. For the inn of
Ashurst is called the Fountain Inn. It is not the Fountain called
the 'Fount of Gold' of which it is written—

> This is that water from the Fount of Gold—
> Water of youth and washer out of cares.

The Fountain of Ashurst runs, by God's grace, with better stuff than water.

Nor is it that other Fountain which is called

> Fountain of years and water of things done.

For though there are honourable years round the Fountain of Ashurst, yet most certainly there are no regrets. It is not done for yet. Binge! Fountain, binge!

Nor is it the Fountain of Vaucluse, nor that of Moulton Parva or Thames-head, which ran dry when George III died and has never run since: nor the Bandusian Spring. No, nor Helicon, which has been tapped so often that it gave out about thirty-five years ago, and has been muddy ever since.

Nor is it of those twin fountains, of hot water the one and of cold the other, where the women of Troy were wont to wash their linen in the old days of peace ere ever Greek came to the land.

No, it was none of these but the plain Fountain of Ashurst, and thither did we plan to send for bread and cheese and for ale with which this fountain flows.

As for whom we should send, it was a selection. Not Grizzle-beard, out of the respect for age, but one of the other three. Not I, because I alone knew the house, and was busy arranging all, but one of the other two. Not the Poet, because, all suddenly, the Muse had him by the gullet and was tearing him. Already he was writing hard, and had verse almost ready for us, and said that this sort of cooking should not be disturbed.

Therefore it was the Sailor who was sent, though he hated the thought of the cold.

He rose up and said: 'When in any company one man is found more courageous and more merry, more manly, more just, and more considerate, stronger, wiser, and much more holy than his peers, very generous also, yet firm and fixed in purpose, of good counsel, kind, and with a wide, wide heart, then if (to mention smaller things) he is also of the most acute intelligence and the most powerful in body of them all, it is he that is made the drudge and the butt of the others.'

With that he left us, carrying a great two gallon can, and soon returned with it full of Steyning ale, and as he put it down he said: 'The Fountain runs, but not with common water. It shall become famous among Fountains, for I shall speak of it in rhyme.' Then he struck the Poet a hearty blow, and asked after the health of his poem.

The Poet. 'It is not quite completed.'

The Sailor (*sitting down near the fire and pouring out the ale*). 'It is better so! Let us have no filling up of gaps. Beware of perfection. It is a will-o'-the-wisp. It has been the ruin of many.'

Grizzlebeard. 'Is there a tune?'

The Poet. 'There is a sort of dirge.'

Myself. 'Begin to sing.'

The Poet—

> Attend, my gentle brethren of the Weald,
> Whom now the frozen field
> Does with his caking shell your labour spurn,
> And turn your shares and turn
> Your cattle homeward to their lazy byres;

The Sailor. 'Oh! Lord! It is a dirge! The man chaunts like old Despair on a fast day! Come let us——'

Myself. 'No, the Poet must end; let him continue.'

The Poet, when he had looked reproachfully at the Sailor, filled his lungs a little fuller than before, and went on:

> Your cattle homeward to their lazy byres;
> Oh! gather round our fires
> And point a stave or scald a cleanly churn
> The while
> With ritual strict and nice observance near,
> We weave in decent rhyme
> A Threnody for the Departing Year.

The Sailor. '"Decent" is bad; and you cannot have a threnody for something that is not dead.'

The Poet (*continuing*)—

And you that since the weary world began,
Subject and dear to man,
Have made a living noise about our homes,
You cows and geese and pigs and sheep and all the crew
Of mice and coneys too
And hares and all that ever lurks and roams
From Harting all the way to Bodiam bend,
Attend!
It is a solemn time,
And we assembled here
Advance in honourable rhyme
With ritual strict and nice observance near
Our Threnody for the Departing Year.
The Year shall pass, and yet again the year
Shall on our reeds return
The tufted reeds to hurrying Arun dear . . .

Here the Poet stopped and looked at the fire.
'Have you made an end?' said the Sailor with a vast affectation
of solicitude.
'I have stopped,' said the Poet, 'but I have not finished.'
'Why, then,' said the Sailor, 'let me help you on,' and he at
once began impromptu:

As I was passing up your landing towns
I heard how in the South a goddess lay.

Then he added: 'I can't go on.'
The Poet—

She ends our little cycle with a pall.

Grizzlebeard. 'Who does?'
The Poet. 'Why, that goddess of his; I shall put her in and
make her wind it up. The Sailor is not the only man here who
can compose off-hand. I promise you . . .

> She ends our little cycle with a pall:
> The winter snow—the winter snow shall reverently fall
> On our beloved lands,
> As on Marana dead a winding sheet
> Was laid to hide the smallness of her hands,
> And her lips virginal:
> Her virginal white feet.

When that dirge had sunk and they, as they sat or lay before the fire, had nodded one by one, sleep came upon them all three, weary with the long day's going and the keenness of the air. They had in their minds, that All Hallowe'en as sleep took them, the Forest of the high-land and the great Weald all spread below and the road downward into it, and our arrival beneath the nightly majesty of the Downs. They took their rest before the fire.

But I was still wakeful, all alone, remembering All-Hallows and what dancing there was in the woods that night, though no man living might hear the music, or see the dancers go. I thought the fire-lit darkness was alive. So I slipped to the door very quietly, covering the latch with my fingers to dumb its noise, and I went out and watched the world.

The moon stood over Chanctonbury, so removed and cold in her silver that you might almost have thought her careless of the follies of men; little clouds, her attendants, shone beneath her worshipping, and they presided together over a general silence. Her light caught the edges of the Downs. There was no mist. She was still frosty-clear when I saw her set behind those hills. The stars were more brilliant after her setting, and deep quiet held the valley of Adur, my little river, slipping at low tide towards the sea.

*

When I had seen all this I went back within doors, as noiselessly as I had come out, and I picked through the sleepers to my own place, and I wrapped myself in my cloak before the fire. Sleep came at last to me also; but that night dead friends visited me in dreams.

THE FIRST OF NOVEMBER
1902

THE FIRST OF NOVEMBER

1902

NEXT morning when I woke it was because the Poet was timidly walking about the room, making as much noise as he dared, but unwilling to be longer alone.

The fire was out, and the small place looked mournful under the grey dawn. I could see through the window that the weather had changed and the air was warmer. All the sky was hurrying cloud, and there would be rain I thought from one time to another on that day. But it would be a good day I thought, for it was All-Hallows, which balances the year, and makes a counter-weight, as it were, to All Fools in her earlier part, when she is light and young, and when she has forgotten winter and is glad that summer is near, and has never heard them at all, or of the fall of leaves.

Grizzlebeard also stirred and woke, and then, last, the Sailor, rather stupored, and all of them looked at me as much as to say: 'Have you no breakfast here?' But I, seeing what was in their minds, met them at once determinedly, and said:

'In this house we breakfast after the fashion of the heroes, our fathers, that is, upon last night's beer, and the bread and cheese of

our suppers. So did they breakfast who fought with De Mont-
fort up on Mount Harry at the other end of the county six
hundred years ago and more, when they had marched all the day
before as it was, and were marshalled against the king with the
morning. Sorely against their will! For there is no fight in a
man until it is past nine o'clock, and even so he is the better for
coffee or for soup. But to-day there is no fighting, but only
trudging, so let us make our breakfast thus and be off.'

They were none of them content, but since I would have it so
and since there was no help for it, they drank that stale beer, a
mug each, with wry faces, and nibbled a little at the stale bread.
Then we left the rest of the loaf and the cheese for the mice, who
keep house for me there when I am away, and frighten off new-
comers by pretending that they are the spirits of the dead.

So we went out through the door and across the little green to a
wobble road that is there, and by a way across the fields to
Steyning, where we should find the high road to Washington and
Storrington and Amberley Bridge, and so over to the country
beyond Arun and the things we knew.

As we went south over those fields, with the new warmth of
the hurrying clouds above us and the Downs growing higher and
higher, the Poet saying what the others had spared to say, began
to grumble. For he said that beer was no breakfast for a man, but
give him rather tea.

The Sailor. 'Poet, I think you must be a vegetarian, and very
probably (like most men of your luxury) you are yet afraid of
your body—a lanky thing, I grant.'

Myself. 'Burn me those men who are afraid of the Flesh!
Water-drinkers also, and caterwauling outers, and turnip
mumblers, enemies of beef, treasonable to the immemorial ox and
the tradition of our human kind! Pifflers and snifflers, and
servants of the meanest of the devils, tied fast to halting, knock-
kneed Baphomet, the coward's god, and chained to the usurers as
is a mangy dog to a blind man!'

The Sailor. 'Come, let us take it up! Hunt me them over the
hills with horn and with hound! Drive them, harry them, pen
them, drown them in the river, and rid me them from our

offended soil! They are the betrayers of Christendom! They are the traducers of those mighty men our fathers, who upon the woodwork of the Table and the Bed, as upon twin pillars, founded the Commonweal.'

Myself. 'Come, Poet, are you not convinced?'

The Poet. 'Of what? That I should have a decent respect for my body?'

The Sailor. 'Respect go hang itself by the heels until it gets some blood into its pale face, and then take a basting to put life into it!'

Grizzlebeard. 'Do you not know, Poet, that by all these anti-belly tricks of yours you would canalise mankind into the trench that leads to hell? For there is nothing that cannot be made to serve the Master of Evil by abuse, nor anything which cannot by a just and reasonable enjoyment be made to glorify God. Have you any lack of pleasure in this rush of the clouds above us? Or does he seem to you a niggler, the fellow that rides the south-west wind?'

The Poet. 'What is all this flood of yours, you three? What have I said about or against the Body?'

Myself. 'Nay, Poet, but we will tell you more than you care to hear! Consider that glorious great tube a gun, whence shells may be lobbed at such as are worthy of the game. Your man that smirks his hatred of war is he that potters into the dirty adventures against the very weak (but by God's providence his aim is damnable), and he is the man that fees lawyers to ruin the poor.'

The Sailor. 'What all this may have to do with the Body I know not. But this I say: Give it due honour—treat it well, keep it with care. It is a complicated thing—you could not have made it, and if you hurt it it is hard to mend . . . Oh, my succinct and honourable Body! I cherish you! you are my friend! I cannot do without you! On the day I have to do without you I shall be all at sea! With the eyes in you do I read books written by women with a grievance, and with the ears of you do I hear the noise of the vulgarians, and with the feet of you do I enter the houses of the rich but fly the presence of fools! Most profitable, consistent, homogeneous, and worthy Body! I salute you; I take comfort in you; I am glad indeed they gave you to me for this brief mortal while! Little Body! Little Body! Believe me, were I wealthy I would cram you with good things! Nor was I ever better pleased than when I heard from a Franciscan in Crawley that when they hang me I shall not lose you altogether, but that you will return to me some time or another;—but when exactly was never fully set down. Anyhow, I shall catch on to you again and recover you very properly set up and serviceable, without bump or boss, a humpless, handsome thing!'

The Poet. 'All this is quite beside the mark, and you have vented upon me nothing but your temper for lack of breakfast. Never in my life have I believed the things which you would have me believe, nor said a word against this vessel which holds my soul as tight as a bottle does a cork, and of which I know so much, but of my soul so little, though my soul is my only companion.'

Grizzlebeard. 'The Body is a business which we all know too well, but the Soul is another matter. For I knew a man once (not of this county) who said there was no soul, and would have proved it. He had once long ago by an apparatus of his tried to prove there was a soul—but the proof was lacking. So next he naturally thought there could be no soul, and he set out to prove *that* on his four fingers and his thumb, without gimcracks, pragmatically, and in a manner convincing to the blind. And he set out with an apparatus to find proof that there was no soul—but that proof was also lacking. So let us have done with all this, and find our way through this tall screen of trees to Steyning, and to the good house that is there, and have something Christian to prepare us for our road. For the Lord knows that Myself and Queen Elizabeth were wrong in making small, stale beer and bread a proper breakfast for a man. Strong beer and beef are the staple.'

The Sailor. 'Besides which All-Hallows is a great feast, and feeding goes with feasting. We will knock at Myself's door when we are next worried by the duty of fasting for some great evil to be atoned, or when ugly Lent comes round.'

When we had got into the town of Steyning, the Sailor, the Poet, Grizzlebeard, and I, we went into the inn, hotel, guest-house, or hostelry, and there very prettily asked as we passed the host that cold meat and ale might be served us in the smoking-room.

But when we got into the smoking-room, the Sailor, the Poet, Grizzlebeard, and I, we were not a little annoyed to see in a corner of the room, crouched up against the fire in a jolly old easy-chair, which little suited his vile and scraggy person, a being of an unpleasant sort. He had a hump which was not his fault, and a sour look which was. He was smoking a long church-warden pipe through his sneering lips. There was very little hair upon his face, though he did not shave, and the ear turned towards us, the left ear, had been so broken that it looked pointed, and made one shudder. The sneer on his lips was completed by the long slyness of his eye. His legs were as thin as sticks, and he had one crossed over the other; his boots had elastic sides to them, and horrible tags fore and aft, and above them were measly grey socks thin and wrinkled. He did not turn nor greet us as we appeared.

It was our fashion during this memorable walk to be courteous with all men and familiar with none—unless you call that familiarity when the Poet threw beer at a philosopher to baptize him and wake him into a new world, as you shall later read.

We therefore sat awkwardly round the edges of the table, the Poet at the end of it opposite to the window that gives on the stable-yard, Myself next to him at the corner, next to me the Sailor, and beyond him Grizzlebeard, who seemed the most contented of us all, and was in no way put out by the blasted being near the fire, but rather steeped himself in memories of his own, and had eyes that looked further than the walls. We, the younger men, drummed our fingers a little upon the table till the beer was brought in, and then began to wonder what wines were kept in so old a house, and the Poet and the Sailor alternately told lies; the Poet telling of rare wines he had found in the houses of the rich, the Sailor talking of wines that never were in ports far off beyond the wide peril of the seas. Grizzlebeard, hearing them confusedly, said that his father had bought a Tokay in 1849 at 204s. the dozen. This also was a lie. And I, to please them, spoke of true wines, notably of that wine which comes from the inside of a goat-skin in Val d'Aran, Sobrarbe, and the roots of Aragon: the vilest and most tonic wine in the world, alive with the power of the goat.

While we thus spoke (in a quiet way so as not to offend) the beer came in, and our talk drifted on to the price of wines, and from that to those who could afford the price of wine, and from that to the rich, and from that to the very rich. And at last the Poet said:

'I should like to be very rich.'

Whereupon, to the annoyance of us all, the nasty fellow next to the fire took his long, silly pipe out of his mouth, blew a little blue wisp of smoke without body in it from his lips, and said:

'Ugh! What do you call very rich?'

The Poet was by nature a hesitating man, and he was frightened by one speaking to him unexpectedly—and one so hideous! So he said vaguely:

'Oh! not to have to think of things; and not to be for ever in the jeopardy of honour; to be able to dip when one liked into one's purse and to pay for what one wanted, and to succour the needy, and to travel or rest at pleasure.' Then he added, as men will who are of infinite imagination and crammed with desires, 'My wants are few.'

He was thinking, perhaps, of a great house upon an eastern hill that should overlook the Mediterranean Sea, and yet be easily in touch with London, and yet again be wholly isolated from the world, and have round it just so many human beings as he might wish to have there, and all at his command.

I, sitting next to him, took up the conversation as in a game of cards, and began:

'That can't be done! When you are wishing for wealth you are by the nature of things wishing for what man allows and controls. You are wishing, therefore——'

'Don't preach!' said the Person by the fire. The Sailor, to make things pleasanter, began hurriedly:

'If I were very rich I should want a number of definite things, as this gentleman said,' waving his hands towards that gentleman to avoid all unpleasantness, which is a way they have in the foc'sle.

'He didn't say it,' I murmured. 'I said it.'

Whereat the Sailor kicked vigorously and wide under the table by way of hint, and caught the Poet, who howled aloud. Then only was the Person by the fire moved to a single gesture. He looked round sharply with his head and a twist of his eyes, not changing a muscle of his body, but glancing as an animal glances, and moving as an animal moves.

'Go on!' he commanded.

The Sailor was a combative man; but he mastered himself, and went on gradually:

'Oh! I should like to give big dinners pretty often and to go to plays.'

Which was a silly sentence, but true enough. He corrected it, adding:

'And I should like to have a jolly little house, and five or ten or twenty or thirty, or perhaps a hundred acres of land; and there would have to be wood upon it. And I should hate to be near a railway, so I would have a motor; and I must have a telephone, but it must not bring people to the place, so I would have a private telephone wire stretching for miles. And one must have water on one's place. And I should like electric light for the offices, but one wants candles for the rooms.'

When he had got thus far the man near the fire jerked his head over his shoulder at Grizzlebeard. The Sailor stopped astonished, and Grizzlebeard, a little frightened I think, said rapidly:

'Really, I don't know! I don't think I want to be very rich. I suppose I am very rich by any good standard. My house has twenty-three rooms in it, counting the old scullery, which is now a cellar. And I have quite four acres of dug garden-land, and undug land not to be counted. I am a gentleman also, and I can put up as many of my friends as care to come and see me. I have four horses, money in the bank, and no debts. I burn my own wood, and build with my own timber; and I quarry my stone out of my own ground. Really I need no more!'

He remembered something, however, and he said:

'It would be a good thing to help the nations. It would be a good thing to enfranchise the nations which are caught in the usurer's hellish web.'

He was silent. Many memories moved in him, but he was too old to think that much could be done with the world; and how could money do much against the abominations of the world?

It was the Sailor who found courage enough to tackle the Johnnie in the chair.

'And what would you do,' he said aggressively, 'if you were very rich?'

The Man in the Chair did not move.

'I am talking to you, sir,' said the Sailor sharply.

'I know that,' snarled the Man in the Chair in an inhuman way. Then, just before the Sailor exploded, he added,

'I should sit here in this chair smoking this pipe with this very tobacco in it and looking at this very fire. *That's* what I should do, and there would be you four men behind me.'

'Oh, you would, would you?' said the Sailor. 'And how do you know that you would be just as you are?'

'Because I am very rich already,' said the Man in the Chair in a low metallic voice, full of dirty satisfaction . . . 'I am exceedingly rich. I have more money than any other man in the large town of the north where I was born. Yes, I'm rich enough.'

He leaned forward towards the fire for a moment, then he took out a card and tossed it to the Sailor.

'That's my name,' he said. And we bade him 'Good day,' and all went out.

We took the road so as not to go through Wiston Park, for though the house there is as good a sight as any in England, why, it was not ours, and we went past that field where the Saint wheeled his mother in a wheelbarrow, and cursed the haymakers, so that it always rains there in mowing time.

For he was, as the phrase goes in those parts, a Holy Man, and had great power. But as he was very poor, no one guessed it. And first, in following God, he sold his motor to buy a brougham, and then he sold his brougham to buy a dog-cart, and then he sold his dog-cart to buy a broken-down, paint-scratched, nasty go-cart; and then, still serving God, not man, he sold his go-cart and his nag and bought a wheelbarrow. For something he must have to take his old mother to church in. Now all this happened in the year of our Lord 713, just after Sussex got the Faith and hundreds of years before she lost it again, and a little before St. Leonard cursed the nightingales.

So he was taking his mother to church in the wheelbarrow when the haymakers laughed at him as he passed, and the Saint said: 'Laugh men, weep heaven.' And immediately there fell on that field only two inches of rain in half-an-hour, and that on the two-day swathes all ready for Tedding, and Lord! how they did curse and swear! And from that day to this, whether hay time come in May month or in June, it rains in the hay time on that one field.

Now when we had gone about a mile from Steyning and had so turned into the Washington Road, the Sailor bethought him of the card, and pulled it out, and there was written—

> *Mr. Deusipsenotavit,*
>
> *Brooks's.*

The Sailor looked at it right away up, and upside down, and sideways, and held it up to the light so as to look through it as well, and then said:

'It is a foreign name.'

Grizzlebeard took it from him, and after a close view of it said:

'It is a Basque name: it is agglutinative.'

And we all went on to Washington, talking of a thousand things.

As we so talked there came over the edge of the high hills that stood like a wall above us, and from the hurrying clouds before the south-west wind, the first drops of rain, and the Poet said:

'What! Must we go forward on this road although it is raining?'

The Sailor. 'Yes, Ninny-lad, most certainly! What else were roads made for but to give a man hard going over wet land?'

The Poet. 'Well, I say there is a time for everything, and rain-time is not the time for walking on a road.'

The Sailor. 'Why, then, you mean that autumn days, such as these, are not to be taken at their full measure, nor to give us their full profit, but that we are to go down to dry death without knowing the taste of Sussex air in the rain?'

The Poet. 'No, I say it aloud, there are days for everything, although we do not know the reason why, and that is why I never will be shaved on a Sunday, for I count it unlucky.

'You may have noticed up and down England some men with nasty undergrowths upon their upper lips alone, and others with great wild beards like Grizzlebeard here, and others with moth-eaten beards as it were—the worst of all; depend upon it they shaved, each of them, at some time or another of a Sunday.

'It is a day of rest, and there is no labour like shaving. It is a day of dignity, and there is no grimacing, sour-faced, donnish occupation like that of shaving. So I say: "There is a day for everything, and everything has its lucky time except burial."'

Myself. 'There now! And that was the very thing I was going to say *had* its most varying days! For does not the old rhyme go:

> Buried on Monday, buried for health,
> Buried on Tuesday, buried for wealth;
> Buried on Wednesday, buried at leisure,
> Buried on Thursday, buried for pleasure;
> Buried on Friday, buried for fun,
> Buried on Saturday, buried at one.'

The Sailor. 'Why?'

Myself. 'There you show yourself what you are, a man that follows the sea. For on land here we knock off work at twelve on Saturday—that is parsons, gravediggers, coffin-carriers, mourners, and the rest, who very willingly dispose of the dead between seven and five of a week day, but do claim their half-holiday. But you sailors may claim your half till you are black in the face, another disposes of your time! And even if a law were

passed that you should loll about from eight bells on Saturday
noon to the dog watch of Monday, as we do on land, that other
would tickle you up with a snorter before you had lit your pipes.
Tumble up there the lot! Watch? I'll watch you, watch or no
watch! Tumble up there and take it lively! Run up and clew
them in till your hands freeze! Pull, you lubbers, pull! Squirm
over the yard like a row of tumblers at a fair, and make fast and be
damned to you! Better for you than for me.

'Then the song goes on (for us jolly people on land; as for you
at sea, you may die and drown as you will):

> Buried on Sunday after eleven,
> You get the priest and you go to heaven.

Grizzlebeard. 'This is rank folly, for absolution is for living
men.'

Myself. 'There you go, Grizzlebeard, verbalising and con-
fumbling, and chopping logic like the Fiend! exegetic and neo-
scholastic, hypograstic, defibulating stuff! An end to true
religion! Soft, old man, soft; the blessing over a coffin does no
man any harm, and is a great solace to uneasy spirits. You are
for ever running into the very gate of heresy with your deter-
minations. It is a bad and a feverish state you have fallen into.
Make amends while you yet have time! Or perhaps when you
come to die you shall have no candles round your coffin and no
large black cloth over it spangled with silver tears, and no bishop
to sprinkle it; nay, who knows, not even a monk nor a parish
priest, nor so much as a humble little curate from the castle.

'When death is on you, Grizzlebeard, I would have you write
out in large black letters on a big white board, 'THIS MAN
BELIEVED,' and hang it round your neck and so die. In this way
there will be no error.

'For errors are made in this matter I assure you, and one man,
though secretly devout (he came from near my own farm), was by
such an error buried anyhow and in common fashion with
prayers only, so that he had to haunt Normans (as they called the
house) on the Dial Post Road. And a job it was, I can tell you!
For the people in that house feared ghosts, and when he walked,

though he walked never so gently, they would give great blood-
curdling shrieks, such as threw him into a trembling and a sweat
—poor spirit!—until the ghost-masters who set the uncomforted
dead such tasks had mercy on him, and let him go haunt the
Marine Parade at Worthing, where no man minded him.'

The Poet. 'Then how was he rested at last?'

Myself. 'Why, in the usual fashion; by the drawing of a
pentagon upon the sand and the sacrificing in its middle of a pure
white hen. I have done.'

The Sailor. 'It is as well, for it has stopped raining.'

And so it had. To our comfort and the changing of our minds.

*

So all along the road under Chanctonbury, that high hill, we
went as the morning broadened: along a way that is much older
than anything in the world: a way that leads from old Pevensey
Port through the Vale of Glynde and across Cuckmere and across
Ouse, and then up to the height of Lewes, and then round the
edge of the Combe, and then down on to the ledge below the
Downs, making Court House and Plumpton Corner, West
Meston, Clinton, and Hollow Pie Combe (though between these
two it branches and meets again, making an island of Wolstonbury Hill), and then on by Poynings and Fulking and Edburton,
and so to the crossing of the water and the Fort of Bramber, and
so along and along all under the Downs until it passes Arun at
Houghton Bridge, and so by Bury and Westburton, and Sutton
and Duncton, Graffham and Cocking, and Diddling and Harting
—all Sussex names and all places where the pure water having
dripped through the chalk of the high hills, gushes out in
fountains to feed that line of steadings and of human homes. By
that way we went, by walls and trees that seemed as old as the old
road itself, talking of all those things men talk of, because men
were made for speech and for companionship, until we came to
the crossroads at Washington; and there, said I to my companions:

Myself. 'Have you heard of Washington Inn?'

Grizzlebeard. 'Why, yes, all the world has heard of it; and when Washington the Virginian, a general overseas, was worriting his army together a long time ago, men hearing his name would say: "Washington? . . . Washington? . . . I know that name." Then would they remember the inn at Washington and smile. For fame is of this character. It goes by the sound of names.'

The Poet. 'For what, then, is the inn of Washington famous?'

The Sailor. 'Not for a song, but for the breeder of songs. You shall soon learn.'

And when he had said that we all went in together, and, in the inn of Washington, we put it to the test whether what so many men had sung of that ale were true or no. But hardly had the Sailor put his tankard down, when he cried out in a loud voice:

'It is true, and I believe!'

Then he went on further: 'Without any doubt whatsoever this nectar was brewed in the waxing of the moon and of that barley which Brutus brought hither in the first founding of this land! And the water wherein that barleycorn was brewed was May-day dew, the dew upon the grass before sunrise of a May-day morning. For it has all the seven qualities of ale, which are:

> Aleph   = Clarity,
> Beth   = Savour,
> Gimel = A lively hue,
> Daleth = Lightness,
> He   = Profundity,
> Vau   = Strength retained,

and lastly, Zayin, which is Perfection and The End.

'It was seeking this ale, I think, that Alexander fought his way to Indus, but perished miserably of the colic in the flower of his age because he did not find it.

'Seeking this ale, I think it was, that moved Charlemagne to ride but North and South, and East and West, all his life long in those so many wars of his whereof you may read in old books; for he lived to be two hundred years and more, and his bramble beard became as white as sea foam and as tangled, and his eyes hollow with age.   And yet he would not abandon the quest for Mitchell's Ale which they sell at Washington: but he could not find it, and so died at last of chagrin.

'And hearing of this ale from a Familiar, Aldabaran sought Saragossa in disguise, and filled ten years full, planning and devising how to get it from the Emir of El Kazar, who was in league with the Evil One; then, in the very moment of his triumph, and as he was unlocking that cellar door, a guardian slave slew him with a sword, and his soul went forth, leaving the cask untasted.

'So also St. Offa, of Swinestead in Mercia, fainting at the thought of this ale which tempting demons had let him smell in a dream, was near to missing his salvation.   He left his cell and went out beyond Kent, over the narrow seas into the Low Countries, and wandered up and down for seven years, until at last he went distracted and raving for lack of the liquor.   But at last he was absolved at Rome.

'Then you have that Orlando, whose fury was aroused by nothing else but a passionate need for this same brew.   For he had led a peaceful life as a cobbler in Upper Beeding until he heard by chance of this ale, and immediately he set out to seek it, and in so doing was led to all his heroic deeds and also to wounds and dissolution at last, and died without ever putting his lips to the tankard.

'Shall I make mention of Gastos or of Clemens?   Of Artaxerxes, of Paulus or Ramon, who all expected and desired this thing in vain?   Or recall Praxiteles or Zeno his cousin, Periscopolos the Pirate, Basil of Cyrene, or Milo?   They also wasted themselves upon that same endeavour.   But to me who am nobler than them all, it has been granted to drink it, and now I know that it resolves all doubts, and I shall go to my great death smiling.   It is the satisfaction of all yearnings, and the true end of all philosophies. Of the Epicurean, for it is a final happiness.   Of the Stoic, for it leaves me indifferent to every earthy thing.   Of the Hegelian, for it is It.   And I see in the depths of it, the conclusion of desire and of regret, and of recollection and of expectation, and of wonder. This is that of which the great poets sang when they said that time itself should be dissolved, of which the chief of them has written:

> Till one eternal moment stops his powers:
> Time being past then all time past is ours.

It is indeed good beer; and when we leave our valleys we will all drink it together in Paradise.'

Grizzlebeard. 'You are right.'

The Poet. 'Yes, you are.'

Myself. 'We are all right together.'

Grizzlebeard. 'It is little wonder that for such as this or worse, the Sons of the Acheans fought ten long years round Troy, or that, nourished by this royal thing, the men of Sussex in old time defeated all their foes, and established themselves firmly upon this ancient land.'

Myself. 'Yes, indeed! Cadwalla, who was the first King of Sussex to learn the true Faith, and who endeared himself for ever to St. Wilfrid and to the Pope, by giving to the one ten thousand, but to the second twenty thousand barrels of this most admirable and impossible-to-be-too-much-praised Cervisian nectar (you may find his tomb in Rome), was moved to extend our power right over sea, even to the Isle of Wight. When he had subdued that land, he took the two princes that were the heirs to its throne, and put them to death. And he conquered all Sussex and all Kent and was mighty before his thirtieth year—all on the ale of Washington. Mitchell's Ale of the Washington Inn! Of such potency it was.'

I looked through the window as I so concluded, and there again had come the storms of rain.

'We will not start,' I said. 'It is raining.'

The Poet. 'But just now . . .'

Myself. 'Oh, Poet! will you also be teasing us with logic, or have you not learnt in your little life how one man may drive off for a game a whole drove of horses, while another may not so much as glance over a little new set maple hedge no higher than his knee? So it is! Let us hear no more of justice and the rest, but sit here snug in the middle of the world, and make

Grizzlebeard do the talking. He has lived longest and knows most, yet has he given us neither a story nor a song.'

'You have told us,' said Grizzlebeard willingly enough, 'the story of Cadwalla, who had that fine imperial instinct in him which made him chafe even within the wide limits of his Sussex kingdom, and sail over the sea with that great expedition of his to conquer and annex the Isle of Wight, the two princes, heirs to which, he also very imperially murdered. Your story made me think of all those other times in history when the armies and the banners of this immortal county have shown themselves in distant lands.'

The Sailor. 'It is interesting that you should know so much, dear Grizzlebeard, but those are far-off things, and we have no true record of them.'

Myself. 'Yet, Grizzlebeard, since you are upon this topic, I very often have much desired to know how it is that this county of ours seems everywhere to exceed its natural boundaries and to have planted a foot north, east, and west in the territory of others; guarding itself, as it were, by bastions and belts of territory not its own, and preserving them as symbols and guarantees of its great military power.'

The Poet. 'Nay, doubtless, the county of Sussex would have expanded southward were it not that it was there contained by the sea, which will brook no man's foot.'

The Sailor. 'Say rather that there was no annexation southward, because the salt sea, being unharvested, there was nothing worth annexing; but, even as it is the fishermen of Sussex will not have foreigners prying about in their preserves, and from the Owers Bank right away to Dungeness, if you will hail a fishing-boat at night he will answer you in the Sussex way. Nor are men of strange seaboards tolerated in that sea.'

Myself. 'I still desire to ask you, Grizzlebeard, since you are the oldest of us, and have in your house so many papers and records, not to speak of in your mind so many ancient traditions of this inviolate land, how is it that Sussex has sovereignty over and beyond the marsh of the Rother, and over and beyond the ridge of hills wherein take their rise the Adur, the Arun, and the

Ouse? For I have often looked at that flat piece without any boundary of its own beyond Crawley, in which all the men seem to be Surrey men, and which I yet notice to be marked Sussex upon the map. How comes it that we are the masters not only of our own rivers, but also of the head waters of the Snouzling Mole, the Royal Medway, and other lesser streams?'

'It so happens,' answered Grizzlebeard, with immense satisfaction, 'that I can answer that question. For this great thing was done at about the time when the tyrant Napoleon was pursuing his petty ambitions among the beggarly nations of the Continent, and it had its origin and spring in that most beloved part of this beloved county whence I also take my being, and where I also was born—I mean the parts round about Hailsham, where the flats invite the sea. There has the fate of our county been twice decided. And since also the full story of the Great Fight has been preserved in the diaries and records of my own family, I am well fitted to tell it to you. For the next few hours I will retail it. Though the rain passes over and the sun comes out, still shall I go on, for it is a favourite of mine. I will go on and on, and relate unendingly the same while you yawn and stretch; nay, though you implore me to cease or attempt to coerce me, yet shall I continue the story until I have completed it.

'You must know, then, that the king who was over Sussex at that time being then in the fortieth year of his age and the twenty-second of his reign, a man not only august but universally loved, and one very tender to the consumers of malt liquor, but a strict governor of brewers (God rest his soul!), a song arose in those parts concerning the tyrant Napoleon and his empty boasting, that when he had conquered Prussia, Russia, Bornesia, Holland, all Italy and Spain, he would challenge the power of Sussex itself before he had done with warfare; and this song, let me tell you, ran as follows.'

With this Grizzlebeard, clearing his aged throat, tunefully carolled out the following manly verse in the tune to which all Sussex songs have been set, without exception, since the beginning of time—the tune which is called 'Golier.'

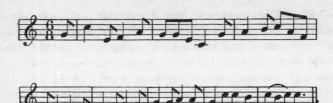

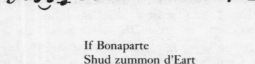

> If Bonaparte
> Shud zummon d'Eart
> To land on Pevensey Level,
> I have two sons
> With our three guns
> To blarst un to the de-e-vil.

'It is,' continued Grizzlebeard, when the long-drawn notes of the challenge had died away, 'a very noble and inspiring song, compared with which "To the North, Merry Boys," is but music-hall blare, and the "Marseillaise" a shrieking on a penny whistle.

'Now this song,' he continued, 'being of its right virtue and glory a hymn that could not but spread far among men, travelled all over our county, being known and commented on in Lewes in the king's own castle, and eastward all along the beach to Hastings, and beyond that to the banks of Brede and over Brede to Rother, which was in those days the boundary of this land; for we had not then begun to give laws to East Guildford, on the left bank of the river mouth.

'As luck would have it, it travelled, perhaps in the speech of pedlars, or printed as a broadside and sold from their packs, all up the valley of Rother and up among the Kentish men, and was soon known in Appledore, Small Hythe, and so on, right up to Goudhurst itself, which stands upon a hill. And here it was that ill-fortune lay in wait for the Kentish men, who had always been a proud lot and headstrong, though relying upon St. Thomas of Canterbury and other worthies, and furiously denying that they had tails. For they had no more humour about them than you will find in a cathedral verger, and so much for Kent.

'Well, then, by the time this great song had come up on to
Goudhurst, where it stands upon its hill, the Kentish men in their
pride and folly, or perhaps only in their ignorance (for I would
not do them wrong), turned it to suit their own purpose and
vanity and had begun to sing it thus:

> If Bonaparte
> Shud zummon d'Eart
> To land on Pevensey Level,
> There are three men
> In Horsemonden
> Will blarst un to the de-e-vil.

'Which corruption and degradation of so great a strain they
very frequently repeated over their cups at evening in the security
of their inland homes.

'Now, when news of this came into Sussex and reached the
king, where he sat in his castle of Lewes, considering his own
greatness and the immensity of the world, he could scarcely
believe his ears. For that the Kentish men should sing songs of
their own and even put on airs when it so suited them, nay,
timorously raid over Rother to pinch a pig when the good-man
was from home, he thought tolerable enough; but that they
should take the song which was, as it were, the very heart of
Sussex, and turn it to their own uses, was, he thought, quite past
bearing, and indeed, as I have said, he could hardly credit it.

'So he very courteously sent a herald mounted upon a little
brown donkey and beautifully apparelled, who came to the King
of Kent, where he sat or rather sprawled at meat in Canterbury.
And this herald, blowing his trumpet loudly in the King of Kent's
ear, delivered him the letter of the King of Sussex, and spurring
round his steed, very gallantly capered away.

'The King of Kent, as you may well believe, was quite unable
to read, but there is no lack of clerks in Canterbury, so he had one
brought, who, trembling, broke open the seal whereon were
stamped the arms of Sussex, and read to his master as follows:

'"Brother Kent: We hear, though we will not believe it, that
certain of your subjects (without your knowing it, we will swear)

have taken to their own use our private anthem, and are singing it wantonly enough in Goudhurst and sundry other of your worthy hamlets; and that, not content with this usurpation of our sovereign right and of the just possessions of our dear people (we are even told, though our soul refuses to entertain it), they have so murdered, changed, and debased this Royal Hymn as to use it in praise of their own selves, and in particular of a steading and sties called Horsemonden, of which neither we nor we think any other man has ever heard.

'"We do you, therefore, to wit, by these presents, brother Kent, that you do instantly command and proclaim by heralds through out your dominions that under pain of horrible torture and death this practice shall immediately cease, if, indeed, we are rightly informed that it has arisen.

'"Greetings and fraternal benedictions.—Given by us in our castle of Lewes on the first day of the October brewing, in the year 3010 since Brutus landed from Troy and laid the foundations of our house.—(Signed) SUSSEX."

'The King of Kent when this message was read to him ordered the unhappy priest to immediate execution (as is the custom in that county when they deal with clerics), but no sooner had he done so than he regretted the act, for not knowing how to write he must needs dictate another letter. So he sent for another priest, who was a long time coming, but when he came bade him write as follows:

'"Brother Sussex, a word in your ear: We may not be book-larned, but we will stand no nonsense, and so sure as hops are hops we will, with some small fragment of our forces, but sufficient to the purpose, come up into your land and harry it, and burn down the steadings and the ricks and carry away all the pigs and cattle; and we will storm your castle, and we will put a new Bishop in Chichester in the place of your Bishop, and we will put our reeves into Midhurst, Horsham, Arundel, and other places, and as for your Royal seat there we will put our own nephew upon it. But as for you we will keep you in chains.—KENT."

'This letter he despatched to the King of Sussex, who when he received it conceived it impossible to avoid war.

'Yet he hoped in his honourable and gentle heart that this last extremity should be avoided, and he sent yet another letter putting it in words even more fair and mannerly than the first, saying that he desired no more than peace with his due rights and honour; and this letter he sent by a herald as he had sent the first. But this second herald the King of Kent put to death, so that now there was no choice but to take arms. So the King of Sussex summoned his army to meet him within fourteen days in the courtyard of the best inn of Lewes, which was in those days called the Turk's Head, but has since been destroyed by those wicked men who hate inns and all other good and lovable things. Marshalling his army there, and seeing to their accoutrements and putting them in good heart, he took the road for Brede, and posted himself upon the height of that hill which has ever since been called BATTLE, facing towards the rising sun.

'The day was the 14th of October, the hearts of all were merry and high, and every man was prepared to do most dreadful things. But how the fight was joined, and how it went, and of the wonderful deeds done in it and of its imperishable effects I must next tell you.'

The Poet. 'I should like to hear the Kentish version of this tale.'

'You must know, then, that the King of Sussex, being thus posted a little before sunrise upon the hill now called Battle, and looking eastward over Brede, he first harangued all his men in proper fashion, and drew them up with skill into a line, urging them whatever they did not to break their rank until they should have defeated the enemy, which, when they had accomplished it, they were free to pursue. And having so spoken he observed coming across the valley the forces of his enemy, the King of Kent, armed with long hop-poles, and carrying themselves in very fierce demeanour. Nay, as they marched they most insolently sang the song which was the cause of all this quarrel; and the Horsemonden contingent in particular, which was in the van, or place of honour, gave forth with peculiar violence the new lines they had composed to their own glory.

'Though this sight, as you may imagine, was malt vinegar and pickles to the men of Sussex, they stirred not a foot, and they said

not a word, but in a grim and determined manner did they turn
up the sleeves of their right arms, spit into their palms, and very
manfully clench their ash-plants, wherewith they did thoroughly
determine to belabour and bang the invaders of their happy
homes.   And there should be mentioned, in particular, the men
of Hailsham, my dear native place, who on that day carried ash-
plants so heavy and huge that ten men of our time could hardly
carry one, though they should stagger under it as builders do
under a scaffolding pole.

'Now the men of Kent began to climb the hill, the men of
Sussex watching them silently from above, and being most
careful in their order to preserve all due regard, and not to walk

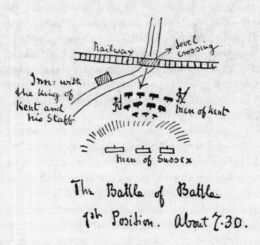

upon the ornamental beds, or to disturb the shrubberies of the
kind gentleman who had permitted them to draw up their line in
the grounds of Battle Abbey.   For in those gardens, note you, is
the position which all the great generals of his staff had pointed
out to the King of Sussex, saying that it was 'a key,' and though
he could make no sort of guess what that might mean, there had
he drawn up his array.

'When the men of Kent felt the steepness of the hill, their song
died away; they began to puff and to blow; and their line, which

they had ordered like so many cattle drovers, was all to pieces, so that while the first of their men, and the leanest, were already approaching the men of Sussex, the last were still tying up their shoe-laces at the bridge, or arguing with the little old man in green corduroy who kept the level-crossing over the railway. For he was assuring them that a train was signalled, and that their advance was most dangerous; but they were protesting that if he would but let them through the wicket gate, which stands by the side of the great railway gates, they could pop across before it came.

'This disarray and grievous lack of generalship in the ranks of Kent was the ruin of that force, seeing that it is laid down in all books of military art that if a line be broken it has lost its strength. But, as you may guess, the art was all on our side, the folly and misfortune upon that of our enemies, whom the God of Battles had already devoted to a complete discomfiture.

'For when the first arrivals of them came to the crest of the hill, all puffed and blown with their climbing, some were banged in the face, others swiped upon the sides, others heavily pushed in the chest, and others more painfully caught upon the point of the chin. Others again were blinded by stout blows in the eye, or turned silly by clever cuts upon the corner of the jaw, whangs upon the noddle, and other tactical feats too numerous to mention. For our king, and yet more his staff, and generals and quartermasters too, were great masters of the art of war. In this skilful manner, then, were the foremost men of Kent sophistically handled, until at last the whole score of them (for the vanguard were at least of that number) broke and ran for cover, and by that action threw into a confusion and stampede the other hundred or so who were still straggling up the hill. Nor was there any heart left in the men of Kent save in the mouths of a few (and their king was one of them), who, having taken refuge in an upper room of the inn that stands by Brede, shouted out mingled encouragement and menace, and bade the fighters in the road below play the man. But these men, considering rather the banging they were getting than the words of their commanders up there in safety, altogether and at one moment fled, bunched into one lump, very frightened and speedy, and spreading rumours that their pursuers were not men but devils. And as they ran they threw their hop-poles down to give them greater speed, and some cast off their coats, and many more lost their hats as they ran, and in general they fell into a rout and confusion.

'As you may imagine, the men of Sussex had by this time the word of command to fall upon them and spare them not at all. Which order they obeyed, belabouring the men of Kent vilely with their ash-plants, and herding and harrying and shepherding them together into the narrow pass of the level-crossing, where they all pushed and screamed, and, especially those on the outer-most part who were the recipients of the ash-plant blessing, showed an immoderate eagerness to be off.

'At last the train of which I spoke having passed, and the little man in green corduroy who kept the level-crossing having con-sented to open the gates, they all poured through in a great stream, tearing for their lives with one half of the men of Sussex after them, pursuing and scattering the foe in every direction, while the other half remained behind in Brede, for a purpose I will presently tell you.

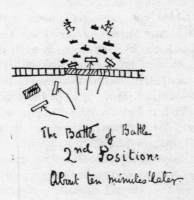

The Battle of Battle
2nd Position.
About ten minutes later.

'The men of Kent then being broken and dispersed all over that countryside, some took refuge in Egham Wood, and others fled to Inkpin, and the more stalwart but not the more brave worked round as best they could to Robertsbridge, while a dozen or more ran to earth in Staplecross. So all that countryside was strewn with hiding and crouching men, some of whom got away and some of whom were taken prisoners, but none of whom re-formed nor showed themselves able to rally.

'Meanwhile their king and his staff, being surrounded in that inn, surrendered upon terms which the King of Sussex in his high and generous heart would not make too hard.

'The first article, then, of this treaty was that for every prisoner released the Treasury of Kent should pay the sum of one shilling, unless he were a Kentish gentleman, and for him the ransom was half-a-crown. And until the money should be paid the prisoners should be held.

'Then the second article was that the men of Kent should pay to the King of Sussex 100 pockets of hops a year by way of tribute, which custom was continued even to our own time, nor did it cease until hops became so cheap that no one would be at the pains of carrying them to Lewes from the Sussex border.

'But the third article, which more concerns us, was that the right bank of Rother from over against Wittersham, so over the canal and then down the wall of Wallingmarsh, and so right to the sea coast, should pass from the Crown of Kent to the Crown of Sussex, and be held by the King of Sussex and his heirs for ever. And so it stands to this day. And to this new frontier land the King of Sussex gave the name of Guildford Level, because it was indeed level, and in honour of the town of Guildford in Surrey, which was his mother's dower. And he built there East Guild-ford, and founded it and endowed it. But it never throve; so that when men talk of Guildford they commonly mean Guildford in Surrey as being the larger of the two towns. And the King of Sussex built a lighthouse in this new province for mariners, and having now both sides of Rye harbour, he deepened it and dredged it so that it became the royal place you know, and far out at sea, where the Fairway begins, he set an old broom fast in the sand by the broomstick, with the besom end of it above the waters, so that no man might miss the Fairway, and there it still stands, a blessing to mariners.

'When the King of Sussex had done all these things he went back home to his castle of Lewes, but not before he had most royally dined and entertained his army in the inn at Battle, and caused to be broached for them 1732 barrels of that exceedingly old ale, called Audit Ale, the memory of which is preserved in those parts most wonderfully.

'This is the story of how the men of Kent were conquered by the men of Sussex and Guildford Level and the marsh were annexed and made a bastion, as it were, of our kingdom. And on account of this great fight it is that Battle is called Battle, and not at all on account of that other skirmish with the Normans, in which we so thoroughly defeated them also, that they turned their backs to the Weald, and ran off as best they could to Dover and the mean places of the East. For we would never have William for our king, and we never did. But he is Duke William for us, and Duke William only now and for ever. Amen!'

The Poet. 'It is possible the men of Kent would tell a different story!'

Myself. 'But that does not tell us the way in which we got hold in this county of all the parts about Crawley, and the belt of land which is very manifestly that of Surrey men.'

Grizzlebeard. 'Why, that was what they call strategical. When the barons of Surrey, the chief of whom lived in a hole under Reigate Hill, heard of the Battle and knew of what stuff the King of Sussex was and all his men, they came of their own accord and asked him to hold that belt of land in which their rivers rise, so as to have better protection. To this he very willingly agreed, and in this fashion was the northern boundary of Sussex drawn.'

Myself. 'And it has stopped raining.'

The Sailor. 'And may it never rain again, for while it rains we sit here in inns and hear nothing but interminable stories.'

When he had said that, we all got up and took the road again, desiring to be in Storrington for lunch, for the weather had a good deal delayed us.

So we went on along that same old road, always westward, until we came to Storrington, and there we went into the inn

called 'The White Horse,' and when we got in there fatigue came
upon us and a sort of gloom, and a quarrelling temper, such as
men will get up between them when they have been penned
together for too long, even if they have been out upon a broad
high road, and have played the part of companions.

As we sat thus together, the Sailor, the Poet, Grizzlebeard
and I, gloomily considering the workedness-out of all things,
and the staleness of experience, there came in quite suddenly
a very tall young gentleman, less than thirty years of age,
lean, and having a thinnish light moustache, more turned
up on one side than on the other. His eyes were kindly
and wild, and from beneath his hat, which was tilted on the
back of his head, appeared over his high forehead wisps of
grey-brown hair. He had on white leather breeches; he was
booted and spurred; his tail coat was grey, with metal buttons
upon it, and round his throat instead of a collar was a soft piece
of cloth, which had once been carefully arranged, but which was
now draggled. It was fastened by a safety-pin made of gold. A
little mud was splashed on his hat, a little less upon his face,
much more upon his boots and breeches.

This Being held himself back as he walked into the room, shut
the door behind him with a great deal of noise, and said
'Evening!' genially. Then he sat down on one of the Windsor
chairs, sighing deeply.

He jumped up again, rang the bell, didn't wait for it to be
answered, put his head through the door, and said, 'Some of the
same!' shut the door, sat down again and laughed.

We were pleased to see him with us, and we suggested that
even so early he had been hunting the fox, which was indeed the
case. I asked him (though I knew nothing of these things)
whether he had a good run, to which he answered, shaking his
head rapidly and biting one of his moustachios:

'No! No! C'r'inly not! . . . Nearly lost me life!'

'I am sorry to hear that,' said Grizzlebeard, who had often
hunted the fox, but now did so no longer. The Poet, the Sailor,
and I sat silent to hear what the newcomer might have to say.
He heaved a deep and contented breath as of a man in port from

stormy seas, leant forward with his lean body, swung his brown gloved hands slowly between his white leather legs and said:

'Wasn't my horse . . . Haven't got a horse . . . Never had one . . .'

Then turning to Grizzlebeard, whom he rightly imagined to be the wealthiest of our group, he said, 'Like riding?'

'Yes,' said Grizzlebeard, thinking carefully, 'I have always liked to ride horses. I like it still in moderation.'

'Ah!' said the stranger wisely, with his head on one side. 'That's it. Now the way you ride 'em doesn't really matter much; it's the kind of horse!'

'Played cup and ball with you?' said I, kindly.

'Contrariwise, he went quite smooth and easy; but oh my Lord, his courage! . . .

'You know,' he went on, tapping his left palm with his right forefinger, 'there's a kind of courage that's useful and another kind that's foolhardy. Now *this* horse (which was old Benjamin's of Petworth) didn't mind danger and he didn't *know* danger; so there was no merit as you may say; but I'm not denying a good thing when I see it, and I tell you he was a hero!'

He sat down again and thought considerably about the horse. There was a sort of lyricism or inspiration in him. He looked up at the ceiling and said, 'Lord! What a brute!' Then he spread his hands outwards, staring at us with his eyes, and said, 'He was red all over, and his eyes were red as well, and he chucked his head up in the air like a big lizard, and he tried to bite his bit in two with his great teeth, and he snarled and spat defiance, and he could never stand on more than two feet at a time, and he changed them ten times a second. It was what they call "dancing." That's how he went on while all the other people were sitting quietly on their beastly great well-fed animals, looking silly. I didn't say anything to him; I didn't feel it was my place; but an ass of an ironmonger man who's been buying land out Graffham way said, "Whoa then! Whoa there!" . . . Silly gheezer! Made the beast perfectly mad . . . He did hate it! . . . and I had no way of telling him it wasn't my fault, though I longed to—from the bottom of my heart. Then old Squire

Powler, who married my aunt Eliza for her money, and butters up my father about his Dowser-man and the wells, came up and asked me where I had got the beast from, and I said "From Hell," and he went away looking like a fool.'

When this excitable young man had said all this, he was afraid (as men of breeding are when they have got quite off the rails) that he had said too much. But Grizzlebeard, who had the kindest of hearts, said genially, 'Oh, there's no harm in old Mr. Powler.' And even I, though I did not know Squire Powler, said I believed that Dowsers were quite genuine, which was the truth and did no harm.

The tall lean man wanted to be silent after his explosion, but Grizzlebeard drew him on, and the young man's own straightforwardness forbade him to be silent. He was bottling up the tale and it must out, so he burst forth again.

'Well, there! The first thing all the other people did was to go after the little dogs across a field or two. And this horse, which was to carry me about, he stood stock still and looked at them as though he thought they were mad. Then he suddenly raced away in a half circle with his head down, and stopped short in front of an oak tree. This annoyed me so much that I leant forward and slapped him on the side of his face. And my word! Didn't he snap round and try to bite my foot! And then he began hopping sideways in a manner most horrible to see and to feel. Now by this time I was wondering what would become of me, and I could fairly have cried, for if he didn't go back into Petworth where somebody could catch him—and that was what I hoped—the only other thing would be to get off and give him a kick in the ribs and let him run, and then I should have to buy him, and Lord knows who'd find the money for that! S'posin' he went and drowned his silly self in Timberley Brook or got hung up on a post? Eh! What?'

This tall, lean young man again thought that he had exceeded, but our sympathetic faces, nay, our appealing eyes, prompted him to continue. He went on more slowly.

'All of a sudden, a long way off, all the little dogs began making those yelping noises of theirs which they do when they get excited, and as I was right high up on this tall animal I could see their white tails wagging out by Burton Rough, a little beyond the Jesuits. I got really interested. . . . What? Then I stopped thinking of anything, because he, this horse I mean, began going as quickly as ever he could, quite straight, and I knew that there was the Rother in between. Oh Lord! You talk of a mouth! . . .

'Now, when you want to pull up a horse that's got too Frenchy, if you take me,' he continued, looking extremely intelligent, and prepared to detail the whole process, 'there're lots of dodges. Some men 'll give a sharp jerk sideways, and try to wrench his head off, and *I* knew a man (he's dead now . . . kind o' soldier) who just pulled and pulled and then suddenly let go. He said *that* was the way. But what *I* do is to saw backwards and forwards right and left 'til he's reg'lar bored and can't stand it. Then he'll stop to see what's the matter. Any horse will. Even if he'd a mouth like an old conscience. 'Least I thought any horse would 'til to-day; but old Benjamin's horse didn't. Never thought an animal could go so straight! Got quite close to the turf and tucked his shins under him somehow, Tirri *Pat*, Tirri *Pat*, Tirri *Pat*, Tirri *Pat*, Tirri *Pat*, so quick, you couldn't tell hardly when he touched and when he didn't. I wasn't able to turn round and look at his tail 'cause I was so anxious, but it must have been standing straight out . . . his neck was, anyway; and I *knew* the Rother was gettin' closer all the time. He didn't take a lep exactly when he got to the hedges, but he just went on gallopin' and they went by from under him. Thought I never saw the old roofs long way off look so quiet! When I came to Mr. Churton's field, the one where the cows are, I thought all of a sudden, "Sposin' there's wire?" It's a measly sort of crinkled hedge, but enough to hide wire. Well, long 'fore I'd remembered, he was past it; and that was the only place you'd have known you were passin' anything. He missed somethin' with one of his hind feet, damn him, but he was off again. Then I saw the Rother, and I thought to myself quite clearly, "Either he'll jump right over this river, and then it'll be a sort o' miracle because it's eight times as far as any horse has jumped before, and it's just as easy to sit that as anything, because it will be just sailing through the air; or else he'll go into the water, and then he won't play the fool any more.' For I'd always heard that when a wild, common, mad horse got into cold water it cured him, same as 't would anybody else. But there! That's just what didn't happen! Neither of 'em! You'll believe me . . . when he got to the brink of that water—wow!—he swerved round like a swallow and made for the high road and Petworth again! An' when he got on the high road he began dancing slowly home and puffing as though he'd done a day's work, and every now and then he'd sneeze . . . My word, what a day!'

'It can't have taken you a day; it's only lunch time yet,' said Grizzlebeard gently.

'No,' said the genial stranger, getting up towards the door and looking over his shoulder. 'Not it! Didn't take twenty minutes!' Then he roared through the door: ''Nother the same!' shut the door again, and went on: 'Twenty minutes 't most! Over b' 'leven! But it filled up the day all right. Haven't been able to think of anything else for hours. And he came back to old Benjamin's as quiet as a lamb, only with that hellish red glint in his eye. And the stable fellow said:

'"You've been takin' it out of 'im!"'

'I was so angry I didn't know what to say; anyhow, I said: "Take your Beelzebub." And the stable boy said quite fiercely: " E ain't Beelzebub, and you've no right to call 'im so out of his name!" So there might have been a scrap, but I was too tired, and I said I'd take something ladylike to ride home with, and I've got it in the stable now, an' I must be getting on. It's late, and I'm very tired.'

We told him one after the other, and then all in chorus, that we were enchanted beyond measure with the description of his day. Grizzlebeard asked him whether he had heard anything of the run, but he shook his head, and the Poet, who had little imagined that such things were possible in English fields, watched them both with some alarm.

Then we all went out with him to the stables to see his beast. There was a halflight in the stables, a gloom, and standing in the stall an extraordinary sheepish-looking thing, very old and fat, with a cunning face, standing hardly fifteen hands, and plainly determined to take easily the last of its pilgrimage upon this earth. The tall, wild-eyed gentleman went to it, patted it gently upon its obese neck, and as he did so he sighed with a deep sigh of satisfaction and of content. We led it out and saw him get on. His legs looked inordinately long. He very cheerily bade us 'Good evenin',' and as he rode out eastward down the road we heard the slapping of his mount's shoes upon the wet surface, as though in spite of her lethargy (for she was a mare) the weight of the rider was too much for her. It was a slow sort of sidling gait that the noise betrayed as it fainted into the distance. If he had suffered from horses that morning, that afternoon he was having his revenge; it was the horse that suffered.

As we stood there in the stable yard talking, a very short ostler of a hard appearance, with the straw of ages in his teeth, came up, and, believing us to be wealthy, hit his forehead hard with the forefinger of his right hand. Grizzlebeard, who loved his country like his soul and was always sincere, and never allowed enough for the follies and vices of men, but believed them better or wiser than they were, said to the ostler with great curiosity: 'I ought to know that young man. He was a nephew of Sir John Powler's, I believe?' The ostler said as smartly as a serpent: 'Yessir! I don't know about that, sir. He's Master Battie, of The Kennels, sir, where his father 'lows him to live, sir. He's back from abroad, sir.'

Grizzlebeard looked down the road gently, thinking of the whole countryside and fixing his man. Then he said a little sadly: 'Oh! that's Batteson; that was the third one, the one his poor mother used to think so much of, and wouldn't send away.'

We all went into the house together, and when we got there Grizzlebeard, after deep thought, said: 'Now what an extraordinary thing that a man brought up like that, as a boy anyhow, should have allowed himself to get on to a horse like that! Who could ride a horse like that?'

The Sailor. 'Why, no one; but let us be up and going. We must not waste this day, but soon we shall get over that lift of land which lies between us and Arun. Let us take the road.'

So we went out and took the Amberley road, and we passed the heath that is there, leaving the pond upon our right, and we passed the little wood of pine trees, and Grizzlebeard said:

'How much taller is this wood! I knew it when I was a boy!'
And I said, 'Yes, and it is taller even for me.'
And the Poet said, 'I know it.'
And the Sailor said, 'I know it too.'
Myself. 'Yes, we all know this landmark, and we all know these ups and downs, and Rackham Mount, and the monastery behind us, and Parham, that great house. For we are on the fringe of the things we know and in a border country as it were. Very soon we shall speak with our own people under our own hills.'

Grizzlebeard. 'In this hour, then, we shall get over the height of land; and the first of us that sees the river Arun must tell the others, and we will arrange for him some sort of prize, since you all three speak in such terms of the valley.'

The Poet. 'We do not speak of it so from any common affection, no, nor from any affection which is merely deep, but because it is our own country, and because the sight of one's own country after many years is the one blessed thing of this world. There is nothing else blessed in this world, I think, and there is nothing else that remains.'

Myself. 'What the Sailor says is true. When we get over that lift of land upon the Amberley road before us we shall see Arun a long way off between his reeds, and the tide tumbling in Arun down towards the sea. We shall see Houghton and Westburton Hill, and Duncton further along, and all the wall of them, Graffham and Barlton, and so to Harting, which is the end where the county ceases and where you come to shapeless things. All this is our own country, and it is to see it at last that we have travelled so steadfastly during these long days.'

The Poet. 'Whatever you read in all the writings of men, and whatever you hear in all the speech of men, and whatever you notice in the eyes of men, of expression or reminiscence or desire, you will see nothing in any man's speech or writing or expression to match that which marks his hunger for home. Those who seem to lack it are rather men satiated, who have never left their villages for a time long enough to let them know the craving and the necessity. Those who have despaired of it are the exiles, and the curse upon them is harder than any other curse that can fall upon men. It is said that the first murder done in this world was punished so, by loss of home; and it is said also that the greatest and the worst of the murders men ever did has also been punished in the same way, by the general exile of its doers and all their children. They say that you can see that exile in their gestures and in the tortured lines of their faces and in the unlaughing sadness of their eyes.'

Grizzlebeard. 'Tell me, Sailor, when you say that thus, coming home, you will be satisfied, are you so sure? For my part, I have travelled very widely, especially in Eastern places (which are the most different from our own), and, one time and another—altogether forty times—I have come back to the flats of my own country, eastward of the Vale of Glynde. I have seen once more the heavy clouds of home fresh before the wind over the Level, and I have smelt, from the saltings and the innings behind Pevensey, the nearness of the sea. Then indeed I have each time remembered my boyhood, and each time I have been glad to come home. But I never found it to be a final gladness. After a little time I must be off again, and find new places. And that is also why in this short journey of ours I came along with you all, westward into those parts of the county which are not my own.'

The Sailor. 'I cannot tell you, Grizzlebeard, whether a man can find completion in his home or no. You are a rich man, and you have travelled as rich men do, for pleasure—which rich men never find.'

Grizzlebeard. 'Nor poor men either!'

The Sailor. 'Well, poor men do not seek it, so they are not saddened, but rich men, anyhow, travel to find it and never find it; then if they return to find it in their homes, why of course they will not find it there either, for a man must come back home very weary and after labour, or some journeying to which he was compelled, if he is to taste home.'

Myself. 'Nevertheless, Sailor, what Grizzlebeard has asked, or rather what he means by asking it, is true. We none of us shall rest, not even in the Valley of Arun; we shall go past and onwards.'

The Poet. 'I think we shall.'

Myself. 'We shall go past and onwards; we shall not be content, we shall not be satisfied. The man who wrote that he had not in all this world a native place knew his business very well indeed, and it is the business of all verse.'

The Poet. 'Nevertheless we know it in dreams. There are dreams in which men do attain to a complete satisfaction, reaching the home within the home and the place inside the mind. And such a man it was, remembering such dreams, who wrote that he had forgotten the name of his own country and could not find his way to it. But this man had in him a sense that soon the name of his own country would be revealed to him, and he knew that when he heard the name he should find the place well enough; it would come back at once to him, as the memory of his love and of the Dovrefjeld came to that man who had brought home the master-maid in the story. He had brought her home from over seas; but later he had forgotten her, from eating human food.

'This man said he forsaw a fateful moment coming, and that he had it like a picture within. He would be in a tavern sitting by himself, and two others would be there talking low together, so that he should not hear. Yet one of these talking low would speak the name of his own country, and when he heard the name of his own country (he said) then he knew that he would rise up, and take his staff and go.

> I will go without companions,
> And with nothing in my hand—

Myself. 'That is a mistake. If he has a staff in his hand he will have something in his hand. I think he put it in for the rhyme.'

The Sailor. 'Do not, do not interrupt the Poet, or he will not be able to continue his poetry; besides which, one is not bound to these things in poetry as one is in arithmetic; it has been proved a thousand times by the human race in chorus.'

Grizzlebeard. 'Go on, Poet.'

The Poet—

> I shall go without companions,
>   And with nothing in my hand;
> I shall pass through many places
>   That I cannot understand—
> Until I come to my own country,
>   Which is a pleasant land!
>
> The trees that grow in my own country
>   Are the beech tree and the yew;
> Many stand together,
>   And some stand few.
> In the month of May in my own country
>   All the woods are new.

The Sailor. 'I believe I know where this place is of which the Poet talks. It is the corner of the hill above the Kennels, between Upwaltham and Gumber.'

The Poet (*angrily*). 'It is nothing of the sort. It is a place where no man ever has been or will be—at least not such men as you!'

Grizzlebeard. 'Do not be angry, Poet; but tell us if there is any more.'

The Poet. 'There is very little more, and it runs like this:

When I get to my own country
   I shall lie down and sleep;
I shall watch in the valleys
   The long flocks of sheep.
And then I shall dream, for ever and all,
   A good dream and deep.

Grizzlebeard. 'That is the point—that is the point. If a man
could be certain that he would sleep and dream for ever, then in
coming back to his own country he would come to a complete
content! But you must mark you how in all the stories of the
thing, even in the story of the homecoming of Ulysses, they do
not dare to tell you all the human things that followed and all the
incompletion of its joys.'

Myself. 'For my part I think you are very ungrateful or very
mystical; or perhaps you have got religion. But at any rate it is
your business and not mine. I say for my part, if I can get back
to that country which lies between Lavant and Rother and Arun,
I will live there as gratefully as though I were the fruit of it, and
die there as easily as a fruit falls, and be buried in it and mix with
it for ever, and leave myself and all I had to it for an inheritance.'

Grizzlebeard. 'Well then, Myself, since you think so much of
your own country, how shall we mark the passage of Arun when
we come to the bridge of it?'

Myself. 'Let us draw lots who shall drown himself for a
sacrifice to the river.'

The Poet. 'Let us count our money—it must be getting low,
and I have none.'

The Sailor. 'No, let us tell (so many years after, no one cares)
the story of the first love each of us had—such of us as can
remember.'

Each of us, lying in his heart, agreed.

When we had given this promise each to the others (and each
lying in his heart) the rain began to fall again out of heaven, but
we had come to such a height of land that the rain and the veils of
it did but add to the beauty of all we saw, and the sky and the
earth together were not like November, but like April, and filled
us with wonder. At this place the flat water-meadows, the same

that are flooded and turned to a lake in midwinter, stretch out a sort of scene or stage, whereupon can be planted the grandeur of the Downs, and one looks athwart that flat from a high place upon the shoulder of Rackham Mount to the broken land, the sand hills, and the pines, the ridge of Egdean side, the uplifted heaths and commons which flank the last of the hills all the way until one comes to the Hampshire border, beyond which there is nothing. This is the foreground of the gap of Arundel, a district of the Downs so made that when one sees it one knows at once that here is a jewel for which the whole county of Sussex was made, and the ornament worthy of so rare a setting. And beyond Arun, straight over the flat where the line against the sky is highest, the hills I saw were the hills of home.

All we four stood upon that height in the rain that did not hide the lights upon the fields below and beyond us, and we saw white and glinting in the water-meadows the river Arun, which we had come so many miles to see; for that earlier happening of ours upon his rising place and his springs in the forest, did not break our pilgrimage. Our business now was to see Arun in his strength, in that place where he is already full of the salt sea tide, and where he rolls so powerful a water under the Bridge and by Houghton Pit and all round by Stoke Woods and so to Arundel and to the sea.

Then we looked at that river a little while, and blessed it, and felt each of us within and deeply the exaltation of return, the rain still falling on us as we went. We came at last past the great chalk pit to the railway, and to the Bridge Inn which lies just on this side of the crossing of Arun.

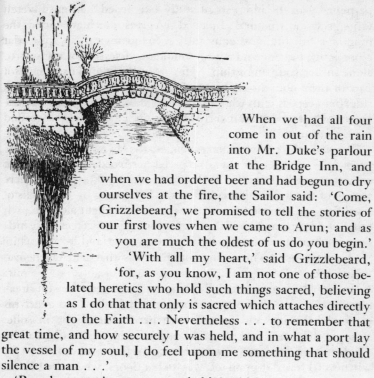

When we had all four come in out of the rain into Mr. Duke's parlour at the Bridge Inn, and when we had ordered beer and had begun to dry ourselves at the fire, the Sailor said: 'Come, Grizzlebeard, we promised to tell the stories of our first loves when we came to Arun; and as you are much the oldest of us do you begin.'

'With all my heart,' said Grizzlebeard, 'for, as you know, I am not one of those belated heretics who hold such things sacred, believing as I do that that only is sacred which attaches directly to the Faith . . . Nevertheless . . . to remember that great time, and how securely I was held, and in what a port lay the vessel of my soul, I do feel upon me something that should silence a man . . .'

'By what moorings were you held?' said I.

'By three,' he answered. 'Her eyelids, her voice, and her name.' Then after a little pause he went on:

'She was past her youth. Her twenty-fifth year was upon her. Her father and her mother were dead. She was of great wealth.

'She had one brother, who lived away in some great palace or other in the north, and one sister who was married far off in Italy. She herself had inherited an ancient house of stone set in her own valley, which was that of the river Brede, and most dear to her; for it was there that she had lived as a child, and there would she pass her womanhood.

'Into this house I was received, for she was much older than I, and when I first knew her I was not yet a man. Thither perpetually in the intervals of study I returned. Insensibly my visits grew most natural; I passed the gates which are the beginning of a full life, and constantly I found myself, in spite of a more active bearing and a now complete possession of my youth, alone in her companionship. Her many servants knew me as a part of their household: her grooms who first had taught me to ride, her keepers with whom I had first shot, her old nurse, a pensioner, who favoured this early friendship. The priest also called me by my name.

'We walked together in long avenues; the lawns of four hundred years were a carpet for us. We paced her woods slowly together and often watched together in the frosty season of the year the early setting of the sun behind bare trees. At evening by her vast and regal fires we sat side by side, speaking in that light alone to each other of dead poets and of the wars and of things seen and of small domestic memories grown to be pictures clear and lovable.

'Then at last I knew what briar it was that had taken root within me.

'In her absence—during the long nights especially—there returned to me the drooping of her eyes: their slow and generous glances. Waking and far off from her, when I saw in some stranger that same rare lowering of the lids I was troubled.

'Her voice, because it was her very self, so moved me, that whenever I heard it upon my way to her doors, whenever I heard it speaking even in the distance no matter what things to another, I trembled.

'Her name, which was not Mary nor Catherine, but was as common and simple a name, was set above the world and was given power over my spirit. So that to hear it attached even to another or to see it written or printed on a page everything within me stirred, and it was as though a lamp had been lit suddenly in my soul. Then, indeed, I understood how truly there are special words of witchcraft and how they bind and loose material things.'

An enthusiasm came into Grizzlebeard's eyes, something at once brilliant and distant like the light which shines from the Owers miles out to sea. He opened his hand down on the table with a fine gesture of vigour, and cried out:

'But what a vision is that! What a spring of Nature even for the poor memory of a man! I mean the unrestricted converse with such a friend at the very launching of life! When we are still without laws and without cares, and yet already free from guardians, and in the full ownership of our own selves, to find a shrine which shall so sanctify our outset: to know, to accompany, and to adore!

'Do not ask me whether I contemplated this or that, union or marriage, or the mere continuance of what I knew, for I was up in a world where no such things are considered. There was no time. No future threatened me, no past could be remembered. I was high above all these things.

'By an accident of fortune I was called away, and in a distant town over seas had alien work put before me, and I mixed with working men. I faithfully curry-combed lean horses, and very carefully greased the axles of heavy wheels, till, after nineteen months, I could come home, and returning I made at once for the Valley.

'As I approached the house I was conscious of no change. The interval had vanished, and I was once again to see and to hear.

'The man that opened the door to me knew me well. I asked for her by her title and her name—for she was noble. He answered me, using her title but not her name. He told me that she would be home that evening late, and he gave me a note to read from her. The writing on that little square of paper renewed in me with a power I knew too well the magic of a sacred place to which I had deliberately returned. As I held it in my hand I breathed unsteadily, and I walked in a fever towards the great gates of iron; nor did I open the letter till I had taken refuge for the next few hours of evening in the inn of her village, where also I was known and had been loved by all in my boyhood.

'There, underneath a little lamp, alone and with food before me, I read the invitation from her hand.

'I learnt in it that she had married a man whose fame had long been familiar to me, a politician, a patriot, and a most capable manufacturer. She told me (for I had warned her of my landing) that they would be back at seven to pass two nights in this country house of theirs, and she begged me to be their guest, at least for that short time.

'A veil was torn right off the face of the world and my own spirit, and I saw reality all bare, original, evil and instinct with death. Nor would I eat and drink, but at last I cried out loud, mourning like a little child; and when I was rested of this I stood by the window and gazed out into the darkness until I had recovered my nature, and felt again that I was breathing common air.

'When spirits fall it is not as when bodies fall; they are not killed or broken; but I had fallen in those moments from an immeasurable height, and the rest of my way so long as I might live was to be passed under the burden to which we all are doomed. Then strong, and at last (at such a price) mature, I noted the hour and went towards the doors through which she had entered perhaps an hour ago in the company of the man with whose name she had mingled her own.'

Myself. 'What did he manufacture?'

Grizzlebeard. 'Rectified lard; and so well, let me tell you, that no one could compete with him.' Then he resumed: 'I entered and was received. Her voice gave me again for a moment some echoes of the Divine: they faded; and meanwhile her face, her person, with every moment took on before me a less pleasing form.

'I have been assured by many who knew us both that what I saw was far from novel. To me it was as strange as earthquake. Her skin, I could now see, though in the main of a sallow sort, was mottled with patches of dead-white (for she disdained all artifice). Her teeth were various; I am no judge whether they were false or true. Her eyes suffered from some affection which kept them half closed; her voice was set at a pitch which was not musical; her gestures were sometimes vulgar; her conversation was inane. I thought in the next quarter of an hour that I had never heard so many things quoted from the newspapers in so short a time.

'But we chatted together merrily enough all three until she went to bed. Then I sat up for some hours talking with the jolly master of the house of politics and of lard. For I had found in my travels and in my new acquaintance with men that every man is most willing and most able to speak of his own trade. And let me tell you that this man had everything in him which can make a good citizen and a worthy and useful member of the State. His intelligence was clear and stable, his range of knowledge sufficient, his temper equable, and his heart so warm that one could not but desire him the best of fates. I have not met him for many years, but I saw in the last honours list that he had purchased a title. I still count him for an older friend.

'Next morning at a hearty breakfast I grew to like him better than ever, and I could see in the healthy light of a new day what excellent qualities resided even in the wife whom he had chosen. The work to which my poverty (for then I was poor) compelled me, called me by an early train to town, and since that morning I have lived my life.

'But that first woman still sits upon her throne. Not even in death, I think, shall I lose her.'

'Grizzlebeard, Grizzlebeard,' said I, 'these things are from Satan! Children and honest marriage should long ago have broken the spell.'

'I am not married,' said he, 'neither have I any children.'

'Then loves here and there should have restored you to yourself.'

He shook his head and answered: 'It was not for lack of them, great or small. There have been hundreds . . . but let us say no more! There was some foreigner who put it well when he said, "Things do not come at all, or if they come, they come not at that moment when they would have given us the fullness of delight."'

There remained in his pewter a little less than half the beer it had held. He gazed at it and noted also at his side, by the fire, a deal box full of sand, such as we use in my county for sanding of the floor.

Steadily, and with design, he poured out all the beer upon the sand, and put down his pewter with a ring.

The beer did not defile the sand. It was soaked in cleanly, and an excellent aroma rose from it over the room. But beer, as beer,

beer meant for men, good beer and nourishing, beer fulfilling the Cervisian Functions, beer drinkable, beer satisfying, beer meet-to-be-consumed: that beer it could never be again.

Then Grizzlebeard said: 'You see what I have done. I did it chiefly for a sacrifice, since we should always forego some part of every pleasure, offering it up to the Presiders over all pleasure and pouring it out in a seeming waste before the gods to show that we honour them duly. But I did it also for a symbol of what befalls the chief experience in the life of every man.'

There was a long silence when Grizzlebeard had done. From where I sat I could look through the window and see the line of the Downs, and the great beech woods, and birds swinging in the rainy air; and I remembered one pair of men and women, and another and another, and then I fell to thinking of a man whom I had known in a foreign place, who at once loved and hated—a thing to me incomprehensible. But he was southern. Then I heard the silence broken by the Poet, who was saying to the Sailor:

'Now it is your turn.'

And the Sailor said, 'By all means if you will,' and very rapidly began: 'My first love lived in the town of Lisbon, after the earthquake and before the Revolution, when I was a lad of seventeen, and already very weary of the sea. She, upon her side, may have been thirty-six or a trifle more, but in that climate women age quickly. Our romance was short; it lasted but five hours. Indeed, my leave on shore was not much longer, for I was serving in the galley, shame be it said; but a boy must earn his living, and rather than be late on board I would have fled to the hills.'

'What was her name?' said the Poet.

'I do not know,' answered the Sailor, 'I did not ask . . . But one moment! . . . I am not so sure that this was my first love . . . I fear the vividness or my recollection has misled me. Unless I am quite wrong,' he went on, musing slowly, 'it was in New-haven, *before* we set sail upon that Lusitanian cruise, that I met my first love, by name Belina . . . or stay! . . . Wrong again, for that was my second ship. Now you ask me and I begin to search my memory, my first love was not there at all, but at a place called Erith, in London River. At least I think so . . .

'Bear with me a moment, gentlemen,' he said piteously, putting his hand to his forehead; 'the years have trampled up my young affection. . . . Yes, it was that woman at Erith, Joan they called her (did the men). Joan! . . . Unless it was that curious and rather unpleasant woman who lived on the far side of Foulness, with her father, and used to row out with fruit and things when the tide was off the mud, and just before the boats waiting to get through the Swin had water enough to weigh anchor . . . It was one of the two I am fairly sure. The younger woman in Goole (for when I was young, though few things of any size went up river as far as that, we did) was, if I remember right, not a Love at all but a mere Consoler——'

The Poet. 'I do not think you are serious; I don't think you understand what you say.'

The Sailor. 'Why, then, since you know better, you can give me your own list; I have no doubt it will do as well as mine, for my memory is very confused upon these matters.'

The Poet. 'I cannot tell you anything about your affairs, and it seems you cannot tell us either; but I can very well describe my own, since I must do so by the terms of our agreement, though I would rather keep silent.

'I was passing in a certain year, just at the end of my school-days, by a path which led between the two lakes at Bringhanger. It is about a mile from the house, and people do not often pass that way, though it is one of the most beautiful places in the world. The first green was upon the trees, but their buds were still so small that one could see the hills near by through their open branches, and the wind, though it was gentle, looked cold upon the surface of the mere, for it was very early morning. Then it was that I saw upon the further shore, mixed as it were with the foliage and half-veiled by reeds, a young woman whom I was not to see again; who she was or by what accident she came there I have never known. I made at once to watch her form as it passed into the boughs of that lakeside and made in the tracery of them a sort of cloud, as I thought, so that I was not certain for a moment whether I had really seen a human thing or no. Immediately, as though she had melted into the trees, she was gone, and I went on my way. But as I wandered, going eastwards towards Arun, this vision grew and fixed itself within my mind, and then for the next days of lonely travel in the County from inn to inn, it became my companion, until at last I took it for my fellow-traveller. I have kept it in my heart ever since.'

The Sailor. 'Great heavens, what a lie!'

The Poet answered angrily that it was no lie, but the Sailor stood his ground.

'It is a lie,' said he, 'and a literary lie, which is the most contemptible of all lies.'

'I cannot prove it,' answered the Poet sullenly. 'I cannot even prove that what I saw was human.'

'No,' said the Sailor, 'you cannot, for you got it in a book, or you mean to put it in a book; but all that kind of talk has no more flesh and blood in it than the rot-talk of the literary men who write about huntin' in Grub Street. Wow! I would not be seen dead in a field with such flimsy stuff.'

'It was then I wrote,' said the Poet dreamily, as though there were no one by, 'five lines which enshrine her memory.'

And as he recited them the Sailor put up first his thumb and then one finger after another, to mark the completion of each line and the rhymes.

> The colour of the morning sky
> Was like a shield of bronze,
> The something or other was something or other.

'The what?' said the Sailor.

'I cannot remember the exact words,' said the Poet, 'and I have never been able to complete that line properly, but I have the rhythm of it in my head right enough;' and he went on—

> Her little feet came wandering by
> The edges of the ponds.

'Now I've got you,' shouted the Sailor triumphantly, '"ponds" does not rhyme with "bronze."'

'Yes it does!' said the Poet, with excitement. 'It's just one of those new rhymes one ought to use. One does not pronounce the "d" in pond. At least,' he added hurriedly, 'not in the plural.'

The Sailor appealed to Grizzlebeard.

'Grizzlebeard,' he shouted, 'the Poet is telling lies and making bad rhymes! Grizzlebeard!'

Then he looked closer and saw that Grizzlebeard was asleep.

But at the shouting of the Sailor, 'Eh? What?' he said, waking with a start, 'have I missed a story?'

'Two,' said I, 'each duller and worse than the last.'

'Then I am glad I slept,' said Grizzlebeard.

Myself. 'You do well to be glad! The Sailor lied about twenty wenches and the Poet lied about one, but the Sailor's lies were the more entertaining of the two, and also, what is not the same, the more possible. They were lying about their first loves, as you may well believe.'

Grizzlebeard (*muttering*). 'Well, well, small blame to them, we all do that more or less. And you, Myself, have you told your story?'

The Sailor (*eagerly*). 'No, he has not, he has shirked it.'

The Poet. 'He has led us on, and he himself has said nothing, which is not fair.'

Myself. 'I was only waiting my turn, and I shall be very happy to tell you those entertaining things. I make no secret of them. *That* is not my religion, thank Heaven.'

At this point I put on such gravity as the circumstance demanded, and looking at my companions in a sober fashion, so that they might expect a worthy revelation, I took from the ticket-pocket of my coat a sovereign, new minted, yellow red, stamped in the effigy of the King, full-weighted, excellently clean and sound. And holding this up between my finger and my thumb, I said:

'Here is my first love! Whom I met when first I came out from the warmth of home into the deserts of this world, and who has ever been absolutely sure and true, and has never changed in the minutest way, but has ever been sterling and fixed and secure. And in the service of this first love of mine I, in my turn, have been absolutely faithful, and from that loyalty I have never for one moment swerved.   Gentlemen, to be faithful in that sort is a rare and a worthy thing!'

Then I put back the sovereign in my pocket, gently and reverently, and taking up the pewter I drank what was left in it, and said to them in more solemn tones:

'You see what I have done. . I have quite drained this tankard. It is empty now.   I did it chiefly because I felt inclined; since it is commonsense that we should never forego any one of the few pleasures which we may find to hand.   But I did it also for a symbol of what jolly satisfaction a man may get if he will do what every man should do; that is, take life and its ladies as he finds them during his little passage through the daylight, and his limping across the stage of this world.   So now you know.'

But Grizzlebeard shook his head and said:

'All these things are follies!   But since the rain is over let us be off again.   It is November: the days are brief; and the light will not last us long.   Let us press forward over Arun, and pursue our westward way beneath the hills.'

*

So we did as he bade us, crossing the long bridge and seeing the water swirling through on the strong brown tide, and so along the causeway, and up the first ride into Houghton, where is that little inn, 'St. George and the Dragon,' at which King Charles the Second, the first King of England to take a salary and be a servant, drank as he fled from Worcester many years ago.   And we went on that ancient way, that hollow way, which the generations and the generations rolling upon wheels and marching upon leather, all on their way to death, have worn down so far below the level of the brown ploughed land.   We went past Bury to Westburton, and still onwards to the place where some dead Roman had his palace built, near the soldiers' road, in a place that looks at a great hollow of the Downs and is haunted by the ruin of fifteen hundred years.   But we did not stop to look at the stone pictures there, nor at that sacred head of Winter wherein this southern lord had bidden his slaves express the desolation of our

cold and of our leafless trees.   We went on through the steep,
tumbled land, down the sharp dip of Bignor, and up the sharp
bank of Sutton: always westward, following the road.   And as
we went, with the approach of evening the wind had cleared the
sky.   There were no more clouds.

And as we went along the Sailor said:

'Poet, it is some time since you tried to give us verse, and I
would not press you, for I know well enough that it is hard labour
to you with that nasty sense of failure all the time.   None the less
I will beg you to try your hand, if only to amuse us, for there is
nothing lightens a road like a song, and we have gone already
many, many miles.'

The Poet.   'With all my heart, since we are now upon the edge
of Burton and its ponds, which, with the trees along them, and
the heathy lands, and the way that the whole setting of them look
at the wall of the Downs, is perhaps the most verse-producing
mile in the world.   Inspired by this let me give you the most
enchanting of songs:

> Oh gay!   But this is the spring of the year!
> The sun——

The Sailor.   'Halt!   Halt at once!   You have gone mad, if
indeed to such brains as yours such dignities are reserved.   Has it
not yet sunk into that corked head of yours that it is All-Hallows?

For though it is notorious that poets neither see what is before them, nor hear, nor smell, but work in the void (and hence their flimsiness), yet, if you cannot see the bare branches and the dead leaves, nor smell autumn, nor catch the quality of the evening, for the Lord's sake write nothing. It would be far better so.'

The Poet. 'I am not writing but singing, and it is my pleasure to sing of spring time. Whether I sing well or no you cannot tell until I have accomplished my little song. But you have put me out and I must begin again.'

Whereupon with less merriment, but full of courage, he took up that strain once more.

> Oh gay! But this is the spring of the year!
>   The sun shall gladden me all the day,
> And we'll go gathering May, my dear,
> And we'll go gathering May;
> For the skies are broad and the throstle is here . . .
>   And we'll go gathering May.

When the Poet had sung this again (and his voice flattened towards the end of the short thing), the Sailor, clasping his hands behind his back, began to move more slowly, and so compelled us to slacken pace. He cast his eyes upon the ground, and for a while was lost beneath the surface. He then quoted in a deep tone, but to himself:

'O God! O Montreal!'

The Poet. 'I don't understand.'

The Sailor. 'No, you would not.'

Grizzlebeard (kindly). 'It is a quotation, Poet. It is a quotation from the poem of an Englishman who went to Montreal one day and found that they had put Discobolos into breeches. Whereupon this Englishman, suffering such an adventure among such Colonials, wrote an ode to celebrate the event, and mournfully repeated throughout that ode, time and again, "O God! O Montreal!"'

Myself. 'Yes, since that time it has passed into a proverb, and is used to emphasise those occasions on which the mind of man has fallen short of its high mission in any department of art.'

The Poet. 'Oh!'

The Sailor (*looking up*). 'Tell me, Poet, did you write that yourself?'

The Poet (*defiantly*). 'Yes.'

The Sailor (*after a short pause*). 'Tell me, Poet, what is a throstle?'

The Poet. 'I don't know.'

The Sailor. 'I thought so. And tell me, Poet, does he come out in the spring?'

The Poet. 'I daresay. Most things do.'

The Sailor. 'Well, well, we won't quarrel; but if you have written much more like this, publish it, and we will have some fun.'

The Poet was now thoroughly annoyed, not being so companionable a man (by reason of his trade) as he might be. For men become companionable by working with their bodies and not with their weary noddles, and the spinning out of stuff from oneself is an inhuman thing.

So I said to him to soothe him:

'I am no judge of verse, Poet, but I think it would go very well to real music. Will you not get some one else to put music to it?'

The Poet answered angrily:

'No, I will not, and since the Sailor thinks it is so easy to write good verse on the spur of the moment, let *him* try.'

The Sailor (*gaily*). 'Why, I can do these things in my sleep. I have written the loveliest things on my shirt-cuff before now, listening to public men at dinners. As also alone in those cells to which the police have sometimes confined me for the hours between revelry and morning, I have adorned the walls with so many little, charming little, pointed little, tender little, suggestive little, diaphanous little Stop-shorts or There-you-are's as would, were they published in a book, make me more famous than last year's Lord Mayor.'

Grizzlebeard. 'Yes, but you have not taken up the challenge.'

The Sailor (*easily*). 'I will do so at once.'

And he rattled out:

When open skies renew the year,
　　And yaffle under Gumber calls,
It's because the days are near
When open skies renew the year,
　　That under Burton waterfalls
The little pools are amber clear,
　　And yaffle, yaffle, yaffle, yaffle,
　　　　　　yaffle under Gumber calls.

Then he went on very rapidly:

'Now that is verse if you like! There you have good verse, pinned and knowled; strong-set verse, mitred and joined without glue! Lord! I could write such verse for ever and not feel it! But I care little for fame, and am at this moment rather for bread and cheese, seeing that we are coming near the Cricketers' Arms at Duncton, a house of call famous for this: that men sit there and eat to get strength for the climbing of Duncton Hill, or, if they are going the other way about, they sit there and eat after their descent thereof.'

The Poet. 'It is all very well, but that verse of yours is not yours at all. It is Elizabethan and water, and let me tell you that the Elizabethan manner can be diluted about as successfully as beer. Mix your ale with water half and half, and give me news of it. So with Elizabethan when you moderns think that you have tapped the barrel.'

The Sailor. 'What you say is not true. This is my own verse, and if you tell me it is in the manner of those who wrote at £40 the go under Queen Elizabeth, I am not ashamed. Many men lived in that reign who wrote with dexterity.'

The Poet. 'Well, then, what is a Yaffle?'

The Sailor. 'Why, it is a real bird.'

The Poet (surlily). 'Yes, like the Great Auk.'

The Sailor. 'No, not like the Great Auk at all; for the Great Auk of whom it is written:

　　Here the Great Auk, a bird with hairy legs,
　　Arrives in early spring and lays its eggs

(and that was written of Beachy Head) is dead. But the Yaffle is alive and is a woodpecker, as you would know if you poets had not all your senses corked, as I have said. For when the woodpecker cries "Yaffle" in the woods, all the world of it, except poets, is aware.

'Moreover, in my song there are no women. One knows your bad poet by an excess thereof; but of this sex in the sentimental manner I have also written, saying in majestic rhyme:

> If all the harm that women do
>   Were put into a barrel
> And taken out and drowned in Looe
>   Why, men would never quarrel!'

Myself. 'How any man can speak ill of women in the same breath with the Looe stream that races through the sea not far from the Owers Light is more than I can understand, seeing that no man hears the name of the Owers Light without remembering that song which was sung to a woman, and which goes:

> The heavy wind, the steady wind that blows beyond the Owers,
> It blows beyond the Owers for you and me! . . .'

The Poet. 'It seems to me you are not of the trade; you are choppy in verse, very short-winded, halting; spavined, I think.'

The Sailor. 'Why! I have sung the longest songs of you all! And since you challenge me, I will howl you one quite rotund and complete, but I warn you, your hair will stand on end!'

Grizzlebeard. 'I dread the Sailor. He is blasphemous and lewd.'

The Sailor. 'Judge when you have heard. It is a carol.'

The Poet. 'But it is not Christmas.'

The Sailor. 'Neither is it spring, yet by licence we sang our songs of springtime—and for that . . . Well, let me seize you all. It has a title—not my own. We call this song "Noël".'

Myself (prettily). 'And I congratulate you, Sailor, on your whimsical originality and pretty invention in titles.'

1 November 1902

The Sailor—

Noël! Noël! Noël! Noël!
A Catholic tale have I to tell!
And a Christian song have I to sing
While all the bells in Arundel ring.

I pray good beef and I pray good beer
This holy night of all the year,
But I pray detestable drink for them
That give no honour to Bethlehem.

May all good fellows that here agree
Drink Audit Ale in heaven with me,
And may all my enemies go to hell!
Noël! Noël! Noël! Noël!
May all my enemies go to hell!
Noël! Noël!

Grizzlebeard. 'Rank blasphemy as I said, and heresy, which is worse. For at Christmas we should in particular forgive our enemies.'

The Sailor. 'I do. This song is about those that do not forgive me.'

The Poet. 'And it is bad verse, like all the rest.'

The Sailor. 'Go drown yourself in milk and water; it is great, hefty howl-verse, as strong and meaty as that other of mine was lovely and be-winged.'

Grizzlebeard. 'What neither the Poet nor you seem to know, Sailor, is that the quarrels of versifiers are tedious to standers-by, so let us go into the Cricketers' Arms and eat as you say, in God's name, and occupy ourselves with something pleasanter than the disputed lyric.'

Myself. 'Very well then, let us go into the Cricketers' Arms, where Mr. Justice Honeybubble went when I was a boy, and there delivered his famous Opinion: his Considered Opinion, his Opinion of permanent value, his Opinion which is the glory of the law.'

'What opinion was that?' said Grizzlebeard, going through the inn door, and we following him.

'I can tell you without much difficulty,' said I, 'if you will listen, but I warn you it is a dull, dull thing. Then, for that matter so was that historical lecture of yours upon the Sussex War. But I listened to that, so now you shall listen to me.'

They sat down not very well pleased, but I assured them that when they had heard it they would understand more law than most. 'For the law,' said I, 'is not the dull subject some think it, but a very fascinating trade, full of pleasant whims and tricks for throwing an opponent. It is not all a routine of thrusting poor men in prison, as is too commonly believed, and as I have notes here of what that great Judge Mr. Justice Honey-bubble, said and did when he harangued the men of Duncton in the Cricketers' Arms twenty years ago, when I was a boy, and as that feat of his is still famous throughout this part of the County, you will do well to listen.' They ordered their beer therefore, and I had mine free, as is the custom of the County for the one who tells the story, and then taking certain notes from my pocket-book, and putting them in order as is necessary when we are to follow technical matters, I gave it them broadside.

'Well, then, Mr. Justice Honeybubble was a man full of sane humour, my friends. He was of a healthy habit of body. He was a man, as are many of the law, who preserved a vigorous gait . into old age, and an expression of alertness in his limbs and his eyes. His face was ruddy, his eyebrows were thick, his white hair was close, and there was plenty of it.

'It was his pleasure to take long walks when his duties gave him leisure, and he especially chose these grassy uplands; and once he came aswinging down by what used to be, but is not, Glatting Beacon, and so through the Combe and the leafless beeches of Burton Hanger to Duncton and the Cricketers' Arms. It was evening, the air was cold and pure. He strode steadily down the steep road, swinging that walking-sick or rather club which was his dearest companion. In such a mood and manner did he enter this inn where we are now. He entered it with the object of eating and drinking something before going on to find the train at Petworth; for in the days of which I speak public refreshment was permitted to all.

'He was delighted to find, in the main room, a gathering; it was of peasants who were discussing a point of difficulty. They respectfully saluted him upon his entrance, for he always dressed with care, and the constant exercise of bullying men who could not reply had given him a commanding manner.

'He stood before the fire surveying them in a kindly but auth-oritative way, and listened closely while they discussed the matter before them; nor was it easy to discover in what precisely their difficulty lay, save that it concerned two disputants, one George, another Roland, and that the matter of it was thus: Two pigs, "Maaster," "Masr" Burt, the change of a sovereign, and Chichester market.

'Roland had put his case not with fire, and had appealed to right being right.

'George had replied in tones of indignation that he was not of that type of character which submits to the imputation of folly.

'Each had reposed his case upon the known personalities and conditions of "Maaster," "Masr" Burt, Chichester market, current coin, and pigs. When, after a little silence, the assembly, deliberating over their mugs, approached the problem, they did so by slowly reciting each in turn at intervals of about thirty seconds the ritual phrases, "Ar!" "That's it," and in the case of the eldest man at the end of the table the declaration native to this holy valley, "Mubbe soa: mubbe noa."

'Mr. Justice Honeybubble, who had himself been compelled upon one occasion to sum up for no less than four hours and twenty-three minutes, took pity upon these his fellow-men, and said:

'"Perhaps, gentlemen, I can be of some use to you: I am, chrm, chrm, accustomed to the weighing of, er, evidence (in the fullest sense of that word), and I have had no little, chrm, experience in matters which have been laid before me, chrm, in, er, another capacity."

'The peasants, who took him for no less than a noble Justice of the Peace, land-owner, and perhaps colonel of some auxiliary force, respectfully acceded to his desire, and were not disappointed when the humane jurist ordered fresh ale for the whole company, including himself. He then sat down in a brown wooden chair with arms, which stood before the fire, crossed his legs, put the tips of his fingers together, and faced his audience with an expression peculiarly solemn which partly awed and partly fascinated the disputants and the areopagus at large.

'Roland and George had just begun to state their case again and to speak both at once and angrily, for they were unaccustomed to forensic ways, when the Judge silenced them with a wave of his large white right hand, and thus gave tongue:

'"We have here," said he, "what lawyers call an issue; that is, a dispute in opinion, or, at any rate, in statement, as to an objective truth. We eliminate all factors upon which the parties are agreed, and *especially*," here he leant forward and clenched his fist in an impressive manner, "all subjective impressions which, however important in themselves, can have *no* place," and here he waved his right arm in a fine sweeping gesture, "before a civil tribunal."

'At this point George, who imagined from the tone of the bench that things were going ill for him, put on an expression of stubborn resolution; while Roland, who had come to a similar conclusion and thought his cause in jeopardy, looked positively sullen. But the Assessors who sat around were as greatly moved as they were impressed, and assumed attitudes of intelligent interest, concentrating every power of their minds upon the expert's exposition of judgment.

'"So far, so good," said Mr. Justice Honeybubble, breathing a deep sigh and drinking somewhat from the tankard at his side. "So far, so good. Now, from the evidence that has been laid before me it is clear that Burt as a third party can neither concur nor enter any plea of Demurrer or Restraint. *That*," he added sharply, turning suddenly upon an old man at the end of the table, "would be Barottage." The old man, who was by profession a hedger and ditcher, nodded assent. "And Barottage," thundered the worthy Judge, "is something so repugnant to the whole spirit of our English law, that I doubt if any would be found with the presumption to defend it!" His electrified audience held their breaths while he continued in somewhat milder tones, "I admit that it has been assimilated to Maintenance by no less an authority than Lord Eldon in his decision of the matter in *Crawford* v. *Croke*. But in the Desuetude of Maintenance, and the very proper repeal of Graham's Act in 1848 . . . or possibly 1849" (frowning slightly) "I am not sure . . . However, the very proper repeal of Graham's Act has left Barottage," and here his voice rose again and vibrated with his fullest tones, "has left Barottage in all his native hideousness, an alien and therefore an iniquitous and a malign accretion upon the majestic body of our English Common Law." At this point a slight cheer from Roland, who saw things brightening, was suppressed by a glance like an angry searchlight from the eye of the Judge, who concluded in full diapason, "Nor shall it have any mercy from me, so long as I have the strength and authority to sit upon this Bench."

'Mr. Justice Honeybubble drank again, and as he was evidently reposing his voice for the moment, the now terrified but fascinated agriculturists murmured profound applause. Their patriotism was moved, the tradition of centuries rose in their blood, and had an appeal been made to them at that moment they would have shed it willingly, however clumsily, in defence of that vast fabric of the Law . . . In a low, regular, and impressive voice which marked the change of subject, Mr. Justice Honeybubble continued:

'"Now, gentlemen, consider the pigs. It often happens, nay, it must happen in the course of judicial proceedings, that our decision relies not only on the balance of human testimony (and you are there, remember, to judge fact, not law), but upon the fitting together of circumstances as to which that testimony relates, and in noting the actions or the situation of things or even of persons incapable in their nature of entering that witness-box" (and here he pointed to a large stuffed fish in a glass case, towards which all his audience turned with one accord, looking round again in a somewhat blank manner) "and telling us upon oath" (the word oath in a deep base) "what they themselves saw and heard in a manner that shall convey the truth, the whole truth, and nothing but the truth. You cannot subpœna a pig——"

'"Ar! zo you zay. Ar!" broke in the excited George, who was now confident that by some trick of cunning he was being deprived of his pigs, "Ar! zo you . . ."

'"Silence!" roared Mr. Justice Honeybubble. "Am I to be interrupted sitting here on this Bench, not even by counsel, but by one of the parties to the case? I trust I may never have to call attention again in the course of my duties to so disgraceful a breach of the immemorial traditions of an English Court of Justice! Snff! . . . I repeat, we cannot subpœna a pig" (he repeated it with stern eyes fixed full on the unfortunate George). "But what we *can* do, gentlemen, is to ask ourselves what in all reasonable probability would have been the case if under those circumstances, neglecting for the moment what has been said relative to any letters or affidavits put in, were it not what the plaintiff has supposed it to be. Chrm!"

'Here, as the intricacy of detail was making the exposition somewhat difficult to follow, all leant forward and summoned their very keenest attention to bear upon the problem.

'"The decision would depend," went on Mr. Justice Honey-bubble in a tone of finality and relief, "upon the conclusion at which you would arrive in the former or in the latter concatenation of events."

'He leant back in his chair, spread out his hands amply towards them, as offering them well-weighed, unbiassed, and unmoved by a tittle, the great body of evidence which he had sifted and arranged with such marvellous skill.

'"It is for you, gentlemen," he concluded, rising, "to say which of the two conclusions in your conscience after all that you have heard is the true one. Remember that if there is the faintest doubt in the mind of any one of you, it is his solemn duty to give the benefit of the doubt to that party in the suit who would have most advantage from it. I believe I have not influenced you in that decision to the one side or to the other. I hope I have not. Certainly I can speak from my heart and say that in this very grave and important business I have tried to preserve and lay before you a general view which should be absolutely impartial; and now I must leave you to your decision."

'With this Sir Thingumbob Honeybubble nodded to all present, seized his staff, and, passing briskly through the door, left them drowned in a tremendous silence. As he went out he had the kindly thought to order the replenishment of their mugs, and so, glancing at his watch, he went at a smart pace down the road past Burton Rough to the station. But he went through the darkness smiling to himself all the way and humming a little tune.

'Now was not that a fine full-fed judge and worthy of being remembered as he is throughout this valley for that famous decision?'

*

When I had told them all this we took the road again, thinking about lawyers and talking of them, and from that the conversation came by an easy stage to moneylenders, and from them again to traitors, and so we passed in review all the principal activities of mankind in the space of about one mile, until we had exhausted every matter, and there was no more to be said.

After this we all fell silent and tailed off, Grizzlebeard going ahead and getting further and further from us in great thoughtful strides, and the Poet about half-way between; but the Sailor and I taking it easy, for it was agreed between us that we should all meet at the next Inn, whatever it might be. That Inn we found no more than two miles along the road.

And when we had picked up the Poet, who was waiting there for us, he told us that Grizzlebeard had gone in about a quarter of an hour before, and that he feared that he must have got into some entertainment, for all that time he had not come out or made a sign; so, said the Poet, we ought all to go in and find him.

So we turned into that little house as in duty bound, seeing that it was five miles since we had last acknowledged the goodness of God in the drinking of ale, which is a kind of prayer, as it says in the motto:

Laborare est orare sed potare clarior,

which signifies that work is noble, and prayer its equal, but that drinking good ale is a more renowned and glorious act than any other to which man can lend himself. And on this account it is that you have a God of Wine, and of various liquors sundry other Gods, that is, Imaginations of men or Demons, but in the matter of ale no need for symbol, only that it is King.

But when we came up to the house, and turned into it, we found that Grizzlebeard, who had gone in already before us, was in that short time deeply engaged with a Stranger who, maugre Heaven, was drinking tea!

There they sat, hardly noticing our entry, and were at it hammer and tongs in an argument.

The Stranger was a measly sort of fellow in a cloak, tall, and with a high voice and words of a cultured kind, and his eyes were like dead oysters, which are unpleasing things; and he and Grizzlebeard, though they had so recently met, were already in

the midst of as terrible a balderdash of argument as ever the good
angels have permitted on this sad earth.

We spoke to Grizzlebeard loudly, but the stranger paid no
attention to us.

We were very much astonished and looked round-eyed at this,
but Grizzlebeard only looked up and nodded. He was too much
caught by the discussion to do more.

'I should meet that,' he was saying, 'by a dichotomy.'

'By a *what*?' said the Sailor.

The Poet. 'By something German, I think.'

But Grizzlebeard, paying no heed to us at all, said to his
earnest fellow: 'Not teleological; You must not think that; but,
if you like, still less ateleological.'

Myself. 'Good, nor ontological I hope, for that is the very
Devil.'

The Stranger, purposely ignoring us, then replied to Grizzlebeard alone:

'The argument cannot be met thus, because though you will
not postulate the reality of time as a process, you must admit it as
a dimension.'

'Not under compulsion!' said the Sailor fiercely.

But Grizzlebeard, as though we three were not there, replied to
the Stranger:

'The word "dimension" is a *petitio elenchi*.'

The Stranger (eagerly). 'There I pin you, that is sheer Monism!'

Grizzlebeard (more eagerly still). 'Not at all! Not at all! On the
contrary, Monism would be your position.'

The Sailor (to the Poet and Myself). 'Let us go hence, my
children, and drink in the bar with common men, for the Devil
will very soon come in by the window and fly away with these
philosophers. Let us be apart in some safe place when the
struggle begins.'

With that we all went out and stayed about ten minutes, drinking with certain labouring men, and paying for their drinks,
because we were better off than they. And to these men we told
such lies as we thought might entertain them, and then, after
about twenty minutes, the Sailor said to us.

The Sailor. 'Those two hateful ones we have left must by this time have come to the foundations of the world, and have thoroughly thrashed it out how it was that God laid down the roots of the hills, and why millstones and the world are round, and even whether they have free will or no: a thing never yet discovered save through the Bastonnade. But come, let us rout them out! I know this philosophy: when men are at it they chain themselves down for hours.'

With that he led us back to the room, and sure enough we heard them still at it hammer and tongs, and Grizzlebeard was saying, leaning forward, and half standing up in his excitement:

'Why then, there you are! With the content of reality expressed in contradictory terms!'

The Stranger. 'There is no contradiction, but a variety of aspect, which is resolved in a higher unity.'

The Sailor (in a solemn tone). 'Grizzlebeard! Darkness will soon fall upon the Weald, and before it falls we must be beyond Graffham, nay, far beyond. So make up your mind, either to differ with this honest gentleman, or to give way to him here and at once. And in any case you are to find your God' (and here he took out his watch) 'within exactly ten minutes from now, for if you do not we will find Him for you in a sudden way. So in ten minutes find us also in the common bar, or perish in your sins!'

Then we all three went out again, and heard from the common bar a singing going on, the chorus of which was Golier, which is indeed the true chorus of all songs, and the footing or underwork of every sort of common chant and roar of fellowship. But when we came in again the poorer men from shyness stopped. Only the Sailor said to them, 'I think we must sing you a new song, which they are singing, out Horsham way, of Duke William; but you must remember it, for I cannot write it down.' And with that he sang at them this verse:

> Duke William was a wench's son,
>   His grandfer was a tanner!
> He drank his cider from the tun,
>   Which is the Norman manner:
> His throne was made of oak and gold,

His bow-shaft of the yew—
That is the way the tale is told,
  I doubt if it be true!

        But what care I for him?
        My tankard is full to the brim,
        And I'll sing Elizabeth, Dorothy,
            Margaret, Mary, Dorinda,
            Persephone, Miriam,
        Pegotty, taut and trim.

The men that sailed to Normandy
  Foul weather may they find;
For banging about in the waist of a ship
  Was never to my mind.
They drink their rum in the glory-hole
  In quaking and in fear;
But a better man was left behind,
  And he sits drinking beer.

        But what care I for the swine?
        They never were fellows of mine!
        And I'll sing Elizabeth, Dorothy,
            Margaret, Mary, Dorinda,
            Persephone, Miriam, Pegotty,
            Jezebel, Topsy, Andromeda.

The Poet. 'To your aid with She-dactyls—

    Magdalen, Emily, Charity, Agatha, Beatrice, Anna,
      Cecilia, Maud, Cleopatra, Selene, and Jessica . . .

The Sailor (*clinching it*)—

        Barbara stout and fine.

Myself (*to the company*). 'Now is not that a good song, and does
it not remind you of Duke William, who so kindly came over here
to this county many years ago, and rid us of north countrymen
for ever?'
One man in the company said that he could not remember this
song, but wished it written down, to which the Sailor answered
that this could not be because it was copyright, but that, God

willing, he would be passing that way again next year or the year after, and then would give it them once more, so that they could have it by heart, and when he had said this, he put down money so that they all might drink again when he had gone, and led us back to the room where the Stranger and Grizzlebeard were. But he took with him a full tankard of beer, and that for reasons which will presently be seen.

For he stopped outside the door behind which we could hear the voices of the disputants still at it with their realities and their contents, and their subjectivities and their objectivities, and their catch-it-as-it-flies, and he said to us:

The Sailor. 'Have you not seen two dogs wrangling in the street, and how they will Gna! Gna! and Wurrer-Wurrer all to no purpose whatsoever, but solely because it is the nature of dogs thus dog-like to be-dog the wholesome air with dogged and canicular noise of no purport, value, or conclusion? And when this is on have you not seen how good housewives, running from their doors, best stop the noisome noise and drown it altogether by slop, bang, douches of cold wet from a pail, which does dis-spirit the empty disputants, and, causing them immediately to unclinch, humps them off to more useful things? So it is with philosophers, who will snarl and yowl and worry the clean world to no purpose, not even intending a solution of any sort or a dis-covery, but only the exercise of their vain clapper and clang. Also they have made for this same game as infernal a set of barbaric words as ever were blathered and stumbled over by Attila the king when the Emperor of Constantinople's Court Dentist pulled out his great back teeth for the enlargement of his jaw. Now this kind of man can be cured only by baptism, which is of four kinds, by water, by blood, and by desire: and the fourth kind is of beer. So watch me and what I will do.'

Then he went in ahead of us, and we all came in behind, and when we came in neither Grizzlebeard nor the Stranger looked up for one moment, but Grizzlebeard was saying, with vast scorn:

'You are simply denying cause and effect, or rather efficient causality.'

To which the Stranger answered solemnly, 'I do!'

On hearing this reply the Sailor, very quickly and suddenly, hurled over him all that was in the pint pot of beer, saying hurriedly as he did so, 'I baptize you in the name of the five senses,' and having done so, ran out as hard as he could with us two at his heels, and pegged it up the road at top speed, and never drew rein until he got to the edge of Jockey's Spinney half a mile away, and we following, running hard close after, and there we found him out of breath and laughing, gasping and catching, and glorying in his great deed.

'Now,' said he, 'I warrant you, Grizzlebeard will come up in good time, and though he will be angry he will be confused.'

Sure enough, Grizzlebeard came up after us, somewhat more than a quarter of an hour behind, and though he was angry, the hill had taken up some of his anger and had blown him, and when he had cursed at the Sailor, and had told him that the Stranger was, in a sense, his guest, the Sailor bade him be at ease, saying that the Stranger was, in a sense, his boredom and intolerable drag, and that had he not done violence we should never have got on the road at all.

'But tell me,' he added, 'did you not settle anything by the time we got away? You had been at it a good hour, and one would think that men could find out in that time whether they had a Maker or no, and what Dimension was and what Degree.'

But Grizzlebeard was surly and would not answer him, and in the slow recovery of his temper the road seemed long enough: more particularly through the Poet, who, thinking to be genial, began to rattle off a judgment of the world and to say that it was a good thing to agree, and also to bend oneself to practical matters; and thence to talking of fanatics, and so to maundering on of authority, and saying that any man could do well with his life if he only had the sense not to offend those who were his superiors on his way upwards, and to pay decent attention to what those in control desired of him.

To this sort of balance Grizzlebeard, being the oldest of us, would have agreed; but in his anger, which, though it was declining, still smouldered, he chose to contradict, and he said in a gruff way:

Grizzlebeard. 'What our fathers called "selling one's soul."
Yes; it is the easiest and the worst thing a man can do.'

The Sailor. 'The worst, perhaps, though I'm not so sure of it,
but the easiest, oh no! And I say I am not so sure it is the worst.
For one never sells anything unless one is hard up, and hard-up
men are never really wicked; it is the rich that are wicked. At
least so I have always been told by the poor, who are not only the
great majority of men and therefore likely to be right, but also
have no interest to serve in saying what they say . . . But easy,
no! Do not tell me it is easy, so long as there stands for a
dreadful example the story of Peter the politician, which all the
world should hear.'

Grizzlebeard. 'And all the world has heard it.'

The Sailor (*sweetly*). 'But not you, Grizzlebeard, so I must give
it at due length to spin the road out and to do you especial
honour.'

Grizzlebeard (*milder*). 'Do so, then. Even your tale may be less
dull than tramping the last hour of a day in silence.'

The Sailor. 'You must know, then, that Peter the Politician,
after having sold every public honour which he could drag upon
the counter and every public office and every kind of power
except his own, and after he had sold his country and his friends
and his father and his mother and even his children, and his self-
respect of course, and all the rest of it, had nothing left to sell but
his very soul. But sell that he must, for have money he must;
without money no man can live the Great Life and go out to dine
in the new hotels that are built out of iron and plaster, and the
Lord have mercy on us all!

'Well then, Peter the Politician did up his soul in a little brown
paper parcel, all beautifully sealed with sealing-wax and tied up
with expensive string; for the public pay for these things where
politicians are concerned.

'He did up his soul, did I say, into this little parcel? I err! It
was his secretary that did it up; not his unpaid secretary—his real
secretary, a humble little man.

'For you must know that politicians have three kinds of
secretaries: the first kind, who may be called Secretarius

Maximus, is a rich man's son, and his place has been paid for: he is called secretary so that he may be advanced to office, and he does nothing at all except ride about in a motor-car and come and sit by when there is any jabbering to be done for his master. Then there is the second kind of secretary, who is usually a friend's son, and may be called Secretarius Minor; he expects no advancement to a politician's future, but only some little job or other in the Civil Service after his years of labour. And his labour is this: to tell the third secretary what he has to do. Now this third secretary, who may be called Secretarius Minimus, receives the sum of thirty shillings every Saturday, and for this he must sweat and toil and be at beck and call, and go to bed late and get up early, and wear himself to a shadow, and then at forty go and be a secretary at less wages if he can get the job, or else hang himself or stand in a row for soup on the Embankment; and there is an end of him.

'Well, then, I say it was this third or working secretary who had done up Peter the Politician's soul in a pretty little parcel, in brown paper paid out of the taxes, with fine red seals paid out of the taxes, and with strong, thin, and splendid string paid out of the taxes; and since the politician was very careful about his soul and it did not weigh much, he took it with him himself and set off to the Devil's office to sell it; and where that office was he knew very well, for he had spent most of his time there while he was a young man, and had served his apprenticeship in another part of the same building.

'When Peter the Politician sent in his card he was received with great courtesy by the Limbo-man who kept the doors, and he was asked to sit down on a chair in a sort of little private outer room where distinguished people await the pleasure of the Head Devil.

'In this little outer room there were one or two books to read about problems, especially marriage, and there were some prints upon the wall which were not well done and which the Devil had taken as a bad debt from a publisher; and there was also a calendar, but there were no Saints' Days marked on it, as you may well believe, but only the deaths of conspicuous people, and Peter the Politician did not study it.

'Now when he had been sitting there for about an hour without the need of a fire, there came in a neat little tight little dressed-up-to-the-nines little Imp in buttons, who was very polite indeed, and told him how sorry His Master was to keep Peter the Politician waiting, but the fact was he was in the midst of a great deal of business. Then the little Imp went out and left Peter the Politician alone—and he waited another two hours.

'At the end of this time another taller and older Imp, dressed not in buttons, but in a fine tail-coat (for he was a Tailed Imp), came in and apologised more than ever and said that His Master the Head Devil was extremely sorry to keep Peter the Politician waiting, but would he kindly send in what his business was, and he hoped it would immediately be attended to?

'Then Peter the Politician answered in his short, dignified way that he had come to sell his soul.

'"Of course! Of course!" said the tail-coated Imp. "Dear me! You must excuse me; we have so much to do to-day that we are really run off our hooves. Of course," he added, anxiously polite, "there is a regular office . . ."

'"Yes, yes, I know," said Peter the Politician as impatiently as his dignity would allow. "I know all about that office, but under the circumstances and seeing that I am known here . . ."

'"Yes, of course!" said the big Imp again, and he went out hurriedly, and Peter the Politician was kept waiting another two hours.

'He hummed a little and he shuffled his feet, and he drummed with his fingers, and he began very seriously to think whether he would not go somewhere else, only he knew of no one out of Hell who wanted his soul. So he sighed at last and continued to wait with as much resignation as he could.

'And after another two hours there came in a very tall, gentlemanly, and deep-voiced Major Devil, who told him how exceedingly sorry he was that His Master should have to keep him waiting, especially now they knew the nature of his business, but the pressure of work that day was really awful! And would Peter the Politician, for this once, be kind enough to send in his offer, because the Head Devil really could not come out?

'So Peter the Politician said severely—

'"Luckily I have brought the goods with me." And he handed the Major Devil his nice little brown paper parcel, and the Major Devil went out apologising.

'Then Peter the Politician was kept waiting another two hours. At the end of it there came in a really superior Devil with his hair parted in the middle and a standup-and-turndown collar, and the accent, and everything. He sat down genially at the same table as Peter the Politician, and leant towards him and said most affably and courteously—

'"My dear sir, my Master is very sorry indeed, but there has been a terrible slump in this sort of thing since August; the bottom is quite knocked out of the market, and—and—well, to tell you straight out, what we want to know is how many you have to offer?"

'"How many!" said Peter the Politician, with a real annoyance unworthy of his rank.

'"Yes," said the suave and really important Secretary Devil (for such he was), "the fact is, my Master says he can't quote for these singly in the present state of the market, but if you could bring a gross . . ."

'At this Peter the Politician got up swearing, and went out, forgetting to take his soul with him, and leaving it there on the table all tied up.

'And that is why some people go about saying that he has lost his soul, for he certainly never sold it; and this should teach you that it is not easy to sell one's soul, though it is exceedingly easy to lose it or to give it away.'

The Poet (*with great interest*). 'This is the very first time I have heard this story!'

Myself. 'It is not the fifteenth that I have heard it. The first time I heard it was from a Yankee, and he told it much quicker and better than the Sailor.'

The Sailor (*angrily*). 'Then you may go back to Yankeeland and hear it there!'

Myself. 'Do not be angry, Sailor, you did your best, and I learned several things I did not know before. For instance, about that calendar; I never knew why the deaths of great men were put down in calendars.'

The Sailor (a little mollified). 'Well, you know now. And you also know that when you want to sell your soul you will have to make up a truck-load before you can get reasonable rates.'

Grizzlebeard. 'I think the Sailor's story is immoral.'

The Poet. 'I think so too, for he talks in a flippant way about things which ought to be talked of respectfully.'

Grizzlebeard. 'No, not on that account; it is immoral because it makes out that souls are of different sizes and values. Now it is well known that souls are exactly equal, and that when you weigh them one against the other they do not differ by a grain of sand, and when you measure them there is not a hundredth of an inch between two of them. And that in value they are all precisely the same. This has been laid down at no less than 572 Synods, three Decisions of the Holy Office, and one Œcumenical Council.'

The Sailor. 'Yes, but not in the four first Councils, and still less at Nicea, so that stumps you!'

Grizzlebeard (solemnly). 'Nicea be damned!'

Myself. 'Very well, by all means, but not Trent I hope, which is a very important one, and to be quarrelled with only at a high risk.'

'No,' said Grizzlebeard, 'not Trent, nor Constance for that matter, though it troubles me more.'

*

Then we fell silent again. The grey evening had advanced as we listened to the Sailor's story, and it was growing cold. We went through the half light and the gloaming until it was upon the edge of darkness, time for the evening meal. And we were so weary with the many, many miles of that day that we agreed together to sleep if it were possible in the same place we might eat at, that is, in the next inn. For we were now near the end of all the road we had to go, being but a mile or two from the County border. And as we went we debated our last feast and our last conversation, our last songs, and our necessary farewells.

'My friends,' said I, 'all men before death make a feast if they

can.   It is an ancient custom, and one well approved by time.
Feast before battle if you can, and before death which may come
in battle.   All such death as comes to men in health, it is well to
feast before it.   Now, with to-morrow morning we shall come to
the end of this little journey of ours, all along the County, all the
way from end to end.   Thus we shall attain, as you may say, the
death of our good time.   For it is agreed between us that when we
come to the Hampshire border we shall separate and see each
other no more.'

The Sailor.   'Yes, that is agreed.'

Myself.   'Well, then, let us make a feast.'

The Poet.   'By all means, and who shall pay?'

Grizzlebeard.   'In general it is I that should pay, for I am the
richest.   We have made no feast in all these days, but since this is
to be a solemn sort of feast, and a kind of Passover (for we are
soon to pass over the boundary into Hampshire), every man must
give his share.'

Myself.   'I am very willing, only if I do so, I must call the food
and drink.'

The Sailor.   'I am not willing at all, but unwilling as I am, most
certainly will I eat nothing and drink nothing to which I am not
inclined.'

The Poet.   'In the matter of eating and drinking I am with you
all, but in the matter of paying I differ from you altogether, for I
have nothing.'

Myself.   'How is this, Poet?   It was only to-day that I saw you
with my own eyes at the Bluebell paying for a mug of beer with a
labouring man.'

The Poet.   'It was my last money, and I did it for charity.'

The Sailor.   'Then now you may have the reward of charity and
starve.'

Myself.   'No, no, there is a way out of these matters which is
quite unknown to children and to savages, but open to men of
intelligence and culture as are we.   It is to do things by way of
paper instead of metal.   A fund shall be formed, each one shall
pay into the fund a piece of paper on which shall be written, "I
will meet one-quarter of the bill," and each man shall sign.   When

this is done, one of us four shall be the financier, and shall pay the bill. Then the paper will be called in, and I will pay, and Grizzlebeard will pay, and the Sailor will pay, but you, the Poet, will not pay, and you will be adjudicated bankrupt.'

Grizzlebeard. 'Yes, your principle is right in the main, but I demur to the simplicity of your last clause. I will not allow the honest Poet to go bankrupt. I will buy up his paper, and he shall be my slave for life, and, if I can so arrange it, his family for a good time after as well.'

The Poet. 'I shall be delighted, Grizzlebeard, and I will pay you my debt in songs.'

Grizzlebeard. 'Not if I know it. You will pay it in cash and at interest, and as to how you shall earn it, that is your lookout.'

Myself. 'Well, anyhow, it is determined that we make a feast, and I say for my part that there must be in this feast bacon and eggs fried together in one pan, and making a great commonalty in one dish.'

The Sailor. 'Excellent; and the drink shall be beer.'

The Poet. 'Besides this, what we need is two large cottage loaves of new bread, and butter, and some kind of cheese.'

Myself. 'Poet, did you not tell me that you were of this County and of this land?'

The Poet. 'I did.'

Myself. 'I think you lied. Who in Sussex ever heard of "some kind of cheese"? You might as well talk in Hereford of "some kind of cider," or in Kent of "some kind of foreigner" coming over by their boats from the foreign lands. I think you must have been out of Sussex, Poet, for many years of your life, and at the wrong time.'

The Poet. 'Why, that is true.'

Myself. 'And, undoubtedly, Poet, you acquired in other counties a habit of eating that Gorgonzola cheese, which is made of soap in Connecticut; and Stilton, which is not made at Stilton; and Camembert, and other outlandish things. But in Sussex, let me tell you, we have but one cheese, the name of which is CHEESE. It is One; and undivided, though divided into a thousand fragments, and unchanging, though changing in place and consumption. There is in Sussex no Cheese but Cheese, and it is the same true Cheese from the head of the Eastern Rother to Harting Hill, and from the sea-beach to that part of Surrey which we gat from the Marshes with sword and with bow. In colour it is yellow, which is the right colour of Cheese. It is neither young nor old. Its taste is that of Cheese, and nothing more. A man may live upon it all the days of his life.'

Grizzlebeard. 'Well, then, there is to be bacon and eggs and bread and cheese and beer, and after that———'

Myself. 'After that every man shall call for his own, and the Poet shall drink cold water. But I will drink port, and if I taste in it the jolly currant wine of my county, black currants from the little bushes which I know so well, then I shall give praise to God. For I would rather drink that kind of port which is all Sussex from vine to vat, and brewed as the Sussex Men brew, than any of your concoctions of the Portuguese, which are but elderberry, liquorice, and boiled wine.'

As we thus decided upon the nature of the feast, the last of the light, long declined, had faded upon the horizon behind the latticework of bare branches. The air was pure and cold, as befitted All-Hallows, and the far edges of the Downs toward the Hampshire border had level lines of light above them, deeply coloured, full of departure and of rest. There was a little mist upon the meadows of the Rother, and a white line of it in the growing darkness under the edges of the hills. It was not yet quite dark, but the first stars had come into the sky, and the pleasant scent of the wood fires was already strong upon the evening air when we found ourselves outside a large inn standing to the north of the road, behind a sort of green recess or common. Here were several carts standing out in the open, and a man stood with a wagon and a landaulette or two, and dogcarts as well, drawn up in the great courtyard.

The lower rooms of this old inn were brilliantly lighted. The small square panes of it were shaded with red curtains, through which that light came to us on our cold evening way, and we heard the songs of men within; for there had been some sort of sale, I think, which had drawn to this place many of the farmers from around, and some of the dealers and other smaller men.

So we found it when we knocked at the door and were received. There was a pleasant bar, and opening out of it a large room in which some fifteen or twenty men, all hearty, some of them old, were assembled, and all these were drinking and singing.

Their meal was long done, but we ordered ours, which was of such excellence in the way of eggs and bacon, as we had none of us until that moment thought possible upon this side of the grave. The cheese also, of which I have spoken, was put before us, and the new cottage loaves, so that this feast, unlike any other feast that yet was since the beginning of the world, exactly answered to all that the heart had expected of it, and we were contented and were filled.

Then we lit our pipes, and called each for our own drink, I, for my black currant port, and Grizzlebeard for brandy; the Poet, at the Sailor's expense, for beer, and the Sailor himself for claret. Then, these before us, we sat ourselves at the great table, and saluted the company. But we were not allowed to make more conversation before an old man present there, sitting at the head of the table, one with a small grey beard and halfshut considering eyes, struck the board very loudly with his fist, and cried "GOLIER"—which appeared to be a sort of symbol, for on his saying this word, all the rest broke out in chorus:

> And I will sing Golier!
> Golier, Golier, Golier, Golier,
> And I will sing Golier!

When this verse (which is the whole of the poem) had been repeated some six times, I knew myself indeed to be still in my own County, and I was glad inside my heart, like a man who hears the storm upon the windows, but is himself safe houseled by the fire. So did I know Hampshire to be stretching waste a mile or two beyond, but here was I safe among my own people by the token that they were singing that ancient song 'Golier.'

When they had sung as many verses of this, our national anthem, as they saw fit, a young man called for 'Mas'r Charles,'

and from an extreme corner of the table there came this answer:
    'If so be as I do carl or be carled upon . . .'
    But he did not finish it, for they all took up very loudly the cry,
'Mas'r Charles, Mas'r Charles,' whereupon the very old man,
rising to his very old feet, put his very old hands upon the table,
bending forward, and looking upwards with a quizzical face full
of years and expectation, said:
    'Arl I can sing were that song o' Californy, that were sixty year
ago,' and he chuckled.   Then said another old man near by:
    'Ar, there you do talk right, Mas'r Charles.   There were
Hewlett's Field, what some called Howlett's Field, which come
to be called "Californy" in that same time when . . .' but the
younger men who could not hear him were calling out:
    'Mas'r Charles, Mas'r Charles,' until silence was created again
by the hammer of the chairman's fist, who very solemnly called
upon Mas'r Charles, and Mas'r Charles in a quavering voice gave
us the ancient dirge:

        I am sailing for America
        That far foreign strand,
        And I whopes to set foot
        In a fair fruitful land,
        But in the midst of the ocean
        May grow the green apple tree
        Avoor I prove faalse
        To the girl that loves me.

        The moon shall be in darkness,
        And the stars give no light
        But I'll roll you in my arms
        On a cold frosty night.
        And in the midst of the ocean
        May grow the green apple tree.

    Here the company, overcome by the melancholy of such
things, joined all together in a great moan:

> Avoor I prove faalse
> To the girl that loves me.

This song so profoundly affected us all, and particularly the
Poet, that for some moments we were not for another, when the
Sailor looking up in an abrupt fashion, said:

'Gentlemen, I will sing you a song, but it is on condition you
can join in the chorus.'

To which the chairman far off at the end of the table answered:

'Ar, Mister, if so be as we know it.'

Then a younger man protested:

'Nout but what we can arl on us sing it arter un,' and this was
the general opinion. So when that fist at the end of the table had
performed its regular ritual, and when also more beer had been
brought as the occasion demanded, the Sailor began to shout at
the top of his voice, and without undue melody, this noble song,
the chorus of which he particularly emphasised, so that it was
readily repeated by all our friends:

> Thou ugly, lowering, treacherous Quean
>   I think thou art the Devil!
> To pull them down the rich and mean,
>   And bring them to one level.
>   Of all my friends
>   That found their ends
> By only following thee.
>   How many I tell
>   Already in Hell,
> So shall it not be with me!

On hearing this last line they all banged and roared heartily,
and shouted in enormous voices:

>   Zo zhall ee not be,
>   Zo zhall ee not be,
>   Zo zhall ee not be wi' me!

which, by zealous repetition, they made a chorus, and one old
fellow that had his chin very nearly upon the table said, 'Aye,
marster! But who is she?'

'Why,' said the Sailor, 'She whom we rail at in this song is that

Spirit of getting-on-ed-ness and making out our life at the expense
of our fellow men and of our own souls.'

'We mun arl get on!   If so be as can!' said a young miller from
down the valley.

'Yes,' said the Sailor shortly, 'but let me tell you they overdo it
in the towns.   I do not blame your way . . . and anyhow the song
must go on,' whereat he began the second verse:

> I knew three fellows were in your thrall,
>   Got more than they could carry,
> The first might drink no wine at all,
>   And the second he would not marry;
> The third in seeking golden earth
>   Was drownded in the sea,
> Which taught him what your wage is worth,
>   So shall it not be with me!

And they all cried out as before:

> Zo zhall ee not be,
> Zo zhall ee not be,
> Zo zhall ee not be wi' me.

Then the Sailor began again:

> There was Peter Bell of North Chappel,
>   Was over hard and sparing,
> He spent no penny of all his many,
>   And died of over caring;
> He saved above two underd pound
>   But his widow spent it free,
> And turned the town nigh upside down,
>   So shall it not be with me!

And again, but more zealously than before, they gave him their
chorus, for they all knew North Chapel, and several wagged their
heads and laughed, and one more aged liar said that he remembered the widow.

But the Sailor concluding sang, with more voice than even he
had given us in all those days:

Then mannikins bang the table round,
　For the younger son o' the Squire,
Who never was blest of penny or pound,
　But got his heart's desire.
　　Oh, the Creditors' curse
　　Might follow his hearse,
For all that it mattered to he!
　　They were easy to gammon
　　From worshipping Mammon,
So shall it not be with me!

And in one mighty chorus they all applauded and befriended him, shouting:

Zo zhall ee not be
Zo zhall ee not be
Zo zhall ee not be wi' me.

'Ar! but that be main right!' said the chief moneylender of that place, his eyes all beaming; and indeed for the moment you would have thought that not one of them but had renounced the ambitions of this world, while the Sailor hummed to himself in a murmur:

And Absalom,
　That was a King's son,
Was hangéd on a tree,
　When he the Kingdom would have won,
So shall it not be with me!

The time had now come when the guests must be going save those who were to sleep in the house that night, and whose cattle were stabled there. But when Grizzlebeard and I asked the host apart whether there were room for us, he said there was not, not even in his barn where many would that night lie upon the straw. But if we would pay our reckoning we might sleep (and he would give us blankets and rugs for it) before that fire in that room.

We told him we would be off early, we paid our reckoning, and so for the third time in those three nights we were to sleep once

more as men sleep in wars, but by this time our
bones were hardened to it.

And when the last man had gone his way to
bed or barn we were left with one candle, and
we made our camp as best we could before
the fire, and slept the last sleep of that good
journeying.

THE SECOND OF NOVEMBER
1902

THE SECOND OF NOVEMBER
1902

I WOKE sharply and suddenly from a dream in that empty room. It was Grizzlebeard that had put his hand upon my shoulder. The late winter dawn was barely glimmering, and there was mist upon the heath outside and rime upon the windows.

I woke and shuddered. For in my dream I had come to a good place, the place inside the mind, which is all made up of remembrance and of peace. Here I had seemed to be in a high glade of beeches, standing on soft, sweet grass on a slope very high above the sea; the air was warm and the sea was answering the sunlight, very far below me. It was such a place as my own Downs have made for me in my mind, but the Downs transfigured, and the place was full of glory and of content, height and great measurement fit for the beatitude of the soul. Nor had I in that dream any memory of loss, but rather a complete end of it, and I was surrounded, though I could not see them, with the return of all those things that had ever been my own. But this was in the

dream only; and when I woke it was to the raw world and the sad
uncertain beginnings of a little winter day.

Grizzlebeard, who had woken me, said gravely:

'We must be up early. Let us waken the others also, and take
the road, for we are near the end of our journey. We have come
to the term and boundary of this short passage of ours, and of our
brief companionship, for we must reach the County border in
these early hours. So awake, and waken the others.'

Then I woke the other two, who also stirred and looked
wearily at the thin, grey light, but rose in their turn, and then I
said to Grizzlebeard:

'Shall we not eat before we start to the place after which we
shall not see each other any more?'

But he said, 'No, we have but a little way to go, and when we
have gone that little way together, we will break a crust between
us, and pledge each other if you will, and then we shall never see
each other any more.'

The others also said that this was the way in which the matter
should be accomplished.

Yielding to them, therefore (for I perceived that they were
greater than I), we went out into the morning mist and walked
through it sturdily enough, but silent, the sounds of our footsteps
coming close into our ears, blanketed and curtained by the fog.
For a mile and second mile and a third no one of us spoke a word
to another. But as I walked along I looked furtively first to one
side and then to the other, judging my companions, whom
chance had given me for these few hours; and it seemed to me
(whether from the mist or what not) that they were taller than
men; and their eyes avoided my eyes.

When we had come to Treyford, Grizzlebeard, who was by
dumb assent at this moment our leader, or at any rate certainly
mine, took that lane northward which turns through Redlands
and up to the hill of Elstead and its inn. Then for the first time
he spoke and said:

'Here we will break a loaf, and pledge each other for the last
time.'

Which we did, all sitting quite silent, and then again we took the road, and went forward as we had gone forward before, until we came to Harting.   And when we came to Harting, just in the village street of it, Grizzlebeard, going forward a little more quickly, drew with him his two companions, and they stood before me, barring the road as it were, and looking at me kindly, but halting my advance.

I said to them, a little afraid, 'Do you make for our parting now? We are not yet come to the county border!'

But Grizzlebeard said (the others keeping silent):

'Yes.   As we met upon this side of the county border, so shall we part before we cross it.   Nor shall you cross it with us.   But these my companions and I, when we have crossed it must go each to our own place: but you are perhaps more fortunate, for you are not far from your home.'

When he had said this, I was confused to wonder from his voice and from the larger aspect of himself and his companions, whether indeed they are men.

'. . . And is there,' I said, 'in all the county another such company of four; shall I find even one companion like any of you? Now who is there to-day that can pour out songs as you can at every hour and make up the tunes as well?   And even if they could so sing, would any such man or men be of one faith with me?

'Come back with me,' I said, 'along the crest of the Downs; we will overlook together the groves at Lavington and the steep at Bury Combe, and then we will turn south and reach a house I know of upon the shingle, upon the tide, near where the Roman palaces are drowned beneath the Owers; and to-night once more, and if you will for the last time, by another fire we will sing yet louder songs, and mix them with the noise of the sea.'

But Grizzlebeard would not even linger.   He looked at me with a dreadful solemnity and said:

'No; we are all three called to other things.   But do you go back to your home, for the journey is done.'

Then he added (but in another voice): 'There is nothing at all that remains: nor any house; nor any castle, however strong; nor any love, however tender and sound; nor any comradeship among men, however hardy. Nothing remains but the things of which I will not speak, because we have spoken enough of them already during these four days. But I who am old will give you advice, which is this—to consider chiefly from now onward those permanent things which are, as it were, the shores of this age and the harbours of our glittering and pleasant but dangerous and wholly changeful sea.'

When he had said this (by which he meant Death), the other two, looking sadly at me, stood silent also for about the time in which a man can say good-bye with reverence. Then they all three turned about and went rapidly and with a purpose up the village street.

I watched them, straining my sad eyes, but in a moment the mist received them and they had disappeared.

*

I went up in gloom, by the nearest spur, on to the grass and into the loneliness of the high Downs that are my brothers and my repose; and, once upon their crest, setting my face eastward I walked on in a fever for many hours back towards the places from which we had come; and below me as I went was that good landscape in which I had passed such rare and memorable hours.

I still went on, through little spinnies here and there, and across the great wave tops and rolls of the hills, and as the day proceeded and the light declined about me I still went on, now dipping into the gaps where tracks and roads ran over the chain, now passing for a little space into tall and silent woods wherever these might stand. And all the while I came nearer and nearer to an appointed spot of which a memory had been fixed for years in my mind. But as I strode, with such a goal in view, an increasing loneliness oppressed me, and the air of loss and the echo of those profound thoughts which had filled the last words we four had exchanged together.

It was in the grove above Lavington, near the mounds where they say old kings are buried, that I, still following the crest of my hills, felt the full culmination of all the twenty tides of mutability which had thus run together to make a skerry in my soul. I saw and apprehended, as a man sees or touches a physical thing, that nothing of our sort remains, and that even before my county should cease to be itself I should have left it. I recognised that I was (and I confessed) in that attitude of the mind wherein men admit mortality; something had already passed from me—I mean that fresh and vigorous morning of the eyes wherein the beauty of this land had been reflected as in a tiny mirror of burnished silver. Youth was gone out apart; it was loved and regretted, and therefore no longer possessed.

Then, as I walked through this wood more slowly, pushing before me great billows of dead leaves, as the bows of a ship push the dark water before them, this side and that, when the wind blows full on the middle of the sail and the water answers loudly as the ship sails on, so I went till suddenly I remembered with the pang that catches men at the clang of bells what this time was in November; it was the Day of the Dead. All that day I had so moved and thought alone and fasting, and now the light was failing. I had consumed the day in that deep wandering on the heights alone, and now it was evening. Just at that moment of memory I looked up and saw that I was there. I had come upon that lawn which I had fixed for all these hours to be my goal.

It is the great platform just over Barl'ton, whence all the world lies out before one. Eastward into the night for fifty miles stretched on the wall of the Downs, and it stretched westward towards the coloured sky where a full but transfigured daylight still remained. Southward was the belt of the sea, very broad, as it is from these bare heights, and absolutely still; nor did any animal move in the brushwood near me to insult the majesty of that silence. Northward before me and far below swept the Weald.

The haze had gone; the sky was faint and wintry, but pure throughout its circle, and above the Channel hung largely the round of the moon, still pale, because the dark had not yet come.

But though she had been worshipped so often upon such evenings and from such a place, a greater thing now moved and took me from her, and turning round I looked north from the ridge of the steep escarpment over the plain to the rivers and the roofs of the Weald. I would have blessed them had I known some form

of word or spell which might convey an active benediction, but as
I knew none such, I repeated instead the list of their names to
serve in place of a prayer.

The river Arun, a valley of sacred water; and Amberley Wild
brook, which is lonely with reeds at evening; and Burton Great
House, where I had spent nights in November; and Lavington
also and Hidden Byworth; and Fittleworth next on, and Egdean
Side, all heath and air; and the lake and the pine trees at the mill;
and Petworth, little town.

All the land which is knit in with our flesh, and yet in which a
man cannot find an acre nor a wall of his own.

I knew as this affection urged me that verse alone would satisfy
something at least of that irremediable desire. I lay down therefore at full length upon the short grass which the sheep also love,
and taking out a little stump of pencil that I had, and tearing off
the back of a letter, I held my words prepared.

My metre, which at first eluded me (though it had been with
me in a way for many hours) was given me by these chance lines
that came:

> . . . and therefore even youth that dies
> May leave of right its legacies.

I put my pencil upon the paper, doubtfully, and drew little
lines, considering my theme. But I would not long hesitate in
this manner, for I knew that all creation must be chaos first, and
then gestures in the void before it can cast out the completed
thing. So I put down in fragments this line and that; and thinking first of how many children below me upon that large and
fruitful floor were but entering what I must perforce abandon, I
wrote down:

> . . . and of mine opulence I leave
> To every Sussex girl and boy
> My lot in universal joy.

Having written this down, I knew clearly what was in my
mind.

The way in which our land and we mix up together and are
part of the same thing sustained me, and led on the separate parts

of my growing poem towards me; introducing them one by one;
till at last I wrote down this further line:

> One with our random fields we grow.

And since I could not for the moment fill in the middle of the
verse, I wrote the end, which was already fashioned:

> . . . because of lineage and because
> The soil and memories out of mind
> Embranch and broaden all mankind.

Ah! but if a man is part of and is rooted in one steadfast piece
of earth, which has nourished him and given him his being, and if
he can on his side lend it glory and do it service (I thought), it will
be a friend to him for ever, and he has outflanked Death in a way.

> And I shall pass [thought I], but this shall stand
> Almost as long as No-Man's land.

'No, certainly,' I answered to myself aloud, 'he does not die!'
Then from that phrase there ran the fugue, and my last stanzas
stood out clear at once, complete and full, and I wrote them down
as rapidly as writing can go.

> He does not die [I wrote] that can bequeath
> Some influence to the land he knows,
> Or dares, persistent, interwreath
> Love permanent with the wild hedgerows;
> > He does not die, but still remains
> > Substantiate with his darling plains.
>
> The spring's superb adventure calls
> His dust athwart the woods to flame;
> His boundary river's secret falls
> Perpetuate and repeat his name.
> > He rides his loud October sky:
> > He does not die. He does not die.
>
> The beeches know the accustomed head
> Which loved them, and a peopled air
> Beneath their benediction spread
> Comforts the silence everywhere;

> For native ghosts return and these
> Perfect the mystery in the trees.
>
> So, therefore, though myself be crosst
> The shuddering of that dreadful day
> When friend and fire and home are lost
> And even children drawn away—
> > The passer-by shall hear me still,
> > A boy that sings on Duncton Hill.

Full of these thoughts and greatly relieved by their metrical expression, I went, through the gathering darkness, southward across the Downs to my home.

TIME. GROWS:
YOUNG. IN. A.
GARDEN

MORE TWENTIETH-CENTURY CLASSICS

Details of other Twentieth-Century Classics are given on the following pages. A complete list of Oxford Paperbacks, including the World's Classics, Oxford Shakespeare, Oxford Authors, Past Masters, and OPUS series, as well as Twentieth-Century Classics, can be obtained in the UK from the General Publicity Department, Oxford University Press, Walton Street, Oxford, OX2 6DP.

In the USA, complete lists are available from the Paperbacks Marketing Manager, Oxford University Press, 200 Madison Avenue, New York, NY 10016.

Dead Man Leading

V. S. Pritchett

Introduction by Paul Theroux

An expedition to rescue a man missing in the Brazilian
jungle becomes a journey of self-discovery for his son.
Conradian in conception, the treatment in the novel of
obsession, verging on madness, is strikingly original.

'a rich, original and satisfying book'—*Spectator*

The Secret Battle

A. P. Herbert

Introduction by John Terraine

First published in 1919, *The Secret Battle* is an account
of the wartime experiences of an infantry officer,
Harry Penrose, as he is tested and brought to break-
ing-point, first in Gallipoli, then with his young wife in
London, and finally in the trenches of France. Without
melodrama or sensationalism, Herbert conveys the
full horror of war and its awful impact on the mind
and body of an ordinary soldier.

'This book should be read in each generation, so that
men and women may rest under no illusion about what
war means.'—Winston Churchill

Elizabeth and Essex

Lytton Strachey

Introduction by Michael Holroyd

Lytton Strachey achieved fame with the publication in 1918 of *Eminent Victorians*; but none of his books brought him greater popular success than his last: this dramatic reconstruction of the complex and stormy relationship between Queen Elizabeth I and the dashing, if wayward, Earl of Essex.

'a brilliant and insufficiently appreciated book'—A. L. Rowse

The Fifth Queen

Ford Madox Ford

Introduction by A. S. Byatt

Ford Madox Ford's vision of the court of Henry VIII brilliantly recreates the struggle between Henry's fifth wife, Katharine Howard, and the tough, unscrupulous Thomas Cromwell for the mind and soul of their King.

'The best historical romance of this century.'—*Times Literary Supplement*
'magnificent'—Graham Greene

His Monkey Wife

John Collier

Introduction by Paul Theroux

The work of this British poet and novelist who lived for many years in Hollywood has always attracted a devoted following. This, his first novel, concerns a chimpanzee called Emily who falls in love with her owner—an English schoolmaster—and embarks on a process of self-education which includes the reading of Darwin's *Origin of Species*.

'John Collier welds the strongest force with the strangest subtlety . . . It is a tremendous and terrifying satire, only made possible by the suavity of its wit.'—Osbert Sitwell

'Read as either a parody of thirties' fiction or just crazy comedy, it deserves its place as a 20th-century classic.'—David Holloway, *Sunday Telegraph*

The Village in the Jungle

Leonard Woolf

Introduction by E. F. C. Ludowyck

As a young man Leonard Woolf spent seven years in the Ceylon civil service. The people he met in the Sinhalese jungle villages so fascinated and obsessed him that some years later he wrote a novel about them. It is his knowledge and profound understanding of the Sinhalese people that has made *The Village in the Jungle* a classic for all time.

'The Village in the Jungle is a novel of superbly dispassionate observation, a great novel.'—Quentin Bell

They were Defeated

Rose Macaulay

Introduction by Susan Howatch

In her only historical novel, the author of *The Towers of Trebizond* skilfully interweaves the lives of Robert Herrick and other seventeenth-century writers with those of a small group of fictional characters.

'To the great enrichment of the English language Miss Macaulay has chosen an historical subject. As a result she has achieved her greatest success—which means she has added something permanent to English letters.'—*Observer*

'One of the few authors of whom it may be said she adorns our century'—Elizabeth Bowen

Seven Days in New Crete

Robert Graves

Introduction by Martin Seymour-Smith

A funny, disconcerting, and uncannily prophetic novel about Edward Venn-Thomas, a cynical poet, who finds himself transported to a civilisation in the far future. He discovers that his own world ended long ago, and that the inhabitants of the new civilisation have developed a neo-archaic social system. Magic rather than science forms the basis of their free and stable society; yet, despite its near perfection, Edward finds New Cretan life insipid. He realizes that what is missing is a necessary element of evil, which he feels is his duty to restore.

'Robert Graves' cynical stab at creating a Utopia is a poetic *Brave New World* filled with much more colour and dreaming than the original *Brave New World* of Aldous Huxley.'—Maeve Binchy

The Aerodrome

Rex Warner

Introduction by Anthony Burgess

Published nearly a decade before Orwell's *1984* shocked post-war readers, *The Aerodrome* is a book whose disturbingly prophetic qualities give it equal claim to be regarded as a modern classic. At the centre of the book stand the opposing forces of fascism and democracy, represented on the one hand by the Aerodrome, a ruthlessly efficient totalitarian state, and on the other by the Village, with its sensual muddle and stupidity. A comedy on a serious theme, this novel conveys probably better than any other of its time the glamorous appeal of fascism.

'It is high time that this thrilling story should be widely enjoyed again'—Angus Wilson

'It is a remarkable book; prophetic and powerful. Many books entertain but very few mange to entertain and to challenge at such a deep level.' *Illustrated London News*

The Unbearable Bassington

Saki

Introduction by Joan Aiken
Illustrated by Osbert Lancaster

Set in Edwardian London, Saki's best-known novel has as its hero the 'beautiful, wayward' Comus Bassington, in whom the author invested his own ambiguous feelings for youth and his fierce indignation at the ravages of time.

'There is no greater compliment to be paid to the right kind of friend than to hand him Saki, without comment.'—Christopher Morley